Moments to Remember

KARL K. STEGALL

Ardara House, Publishers
Pensacola, Florida

ISBN 1888676-11-6
Library of Congress Control Number 2006940644

To Brenda

Table of Contents

Preface

REMEMBER!

One of the greatest words found throughout the Bible is the word, *"Remember!"* Down through the centuries, the ancient Hebrews reflected upon the Biblical admonitions,

> *"Remember your Creator in the days of your youth . . ."*
> (Ecclesiastes 12:1)

> *"Remember the Sabbath Day, to keep it holy . . ."*
> (Exodus 20:8 KJV)

> *"Remember that you were slaves in Egypt . . . ."*
> (Deuteronomy 5:15)

When Jesus Christ instituted the sacrament of the Lord's Supper, He knew that our memories, at best, were short. As He gave thanks for the bread and wine and instituted a feast of memory, Jesus said to His disciples *". . . do this in remembrance of me."* (Luke 22:19)

There is nothing more beautiful in all the world than a good memory. During the 1950s, there was a very popular song that was on the hearts and minds of millions of people across our nation. The song was entitled, *"Moments to Remember"* and it

7

was recorded by the Four Lads, Barry Manilow, Johnny Cash, and the Platters.

Some of the lyrics, written by Al Stillman, called attention to special memories in life:

Though summer turns to winter and the present disappears,
The laughter we were glad to share
will echo through the years.
When other nights and other days
may find us gone our separate ways,
we will have these moments to remember.

Over the past twenty-three-and-a-half years, I have been given the great privilege of writing the front cover of the *Tower Chimes*, the newsletter of First United Methodist Church of Montgomery, Alabama. Faithful members asked me to put together in this book a selection of these weekly articles. My prayer for you is that, perhaps, one of these articles might inspire you to remember some very special person or moment within your life.

Karl K. Stegall
Montgomery, Alabama
December 28, 2006

Chapter One

Memories of Home

I'm Thankful..."

...for a wonderful family—a loving wife, Brenda; two beautiful daughters, Stacie and Carmen; a splendid son-in-law, Kevin Haynes; and three marvelous grandchildren, Hannah, Mary Carmen, and Karlson.

...for a small membership church in Emelle, Alabama, that taught me the love of Jesus Christ.

...for growing up in a small community where life was simple, values were clear, and all adults within the community felt they had the right and responsibility to discipline me.

...for the memory of dirt roads, country stores, faded Coke signs, nail kegs, funeral home fans, Burma Shave signs, smokehouses, old barns, rocking chairs on front porches, and a slower lifestyle that they represented.

...for parents who affirm their children with the simple words, *"I love you"* and *"I am proud of you!"*

...for family scrapbooks, personal letters, and telephone calls from old friends.

...for hymns like "Amazing Grace," "The Old Rugged Cross," "How Great Thou Art," and "Great Is Thy Faithfulness."

...for military personnel, police officers, and firefighters.

...for Broadway plays like "Les Miserables" and "Phantom of the Opera."

...for Christmas Eve Candlelight Services and Patriotic Concerts.

...for a Jewish immigrant, Irving Berlin, who composed "I'm Dreaming of A White Christmas," "Easter Parade," and "God Bless America."

...for a crowded sanctuary and the sound of a majestic pipe organ.

...for the marvelous promise found in Romans 8:28, *"And we know that in all things God works for the good of those who love Him, who have been called according to His purpose."*

...for the joy of serving twenty-three-and-a-half years as the senior minister of First United Methodist Church of Montgomery.

The Old Home Place

My oldest brother, Joe, informed me today that our old home place will be sold this week. It was there that I was born in the front bedroom, and I must admit that every inch of that home has a very special memory for me. Since our old home place has been a part of my entire life there are so many precious memories flooding my soul today.

I remember when I was a small child how our family would gather around the table in the dining room for "*supper.*" Following the evening meal, our father made us become very quiet. He would turn on our family radio every evening during those days of World War II, and the first voice we heard was the voice of Gabriel Heater, *"I have good news for you tonight."*

I remember the small kitchen and the gas stove, but more especially, the small table on which my mother kept her Bible and her teacher's manual for the International Sunday School lesson that she taught each Sunday.

I remember my father and mother's bedroom near the center of the house where they could keep a check on us all hours of the night. I remember my mother's trunk beside her bed where, in later years, she neatly stacked every single newsletter from every church that I ever served. She bound them with strings and placed them there.

I remember a little picture hanging on the wall that my father had ordered from Boys' Town, Nebraska. It was that familiar picture of the teenage boy holding his younger brother on his shoulders. Underneath were the familiar words, "*He ain't heavy, father; he's my brother.*" I guess my father thought those good words would "*rub off*" on his five sons.

I remember the living room and table on which my mother kept pictures of all of her children, grandchildren, and great-grandchildren. The pictures always appeared somewhat "dated," to say the least, but then I realized that a mother's love does not change through the years.

I remember the well out back where we would let down a large bucket to get our "*drinking water.*" As a fourth-born, it now seems as though I had more than my share of trips to that well to "draw water" on cold winter nights.

Our old home place will sell this week for such a modest price when compared to the rich memories that will live in my heart forever. I know that when I pass by our old home place again that I will have a strong desire to go back inside and relive some of my precious memories. While that will be impossible, I will be comforted by the Biblical truth that all of us are truly pilgrims on this earth, and our eyes should always be focused on "*a home not made with hands, but eternal in the heavens!*"

13

Oh, How I Miss Joe Rumore!

When I was a little boy growing up in west Alabama, I became a regular listener to Joe Rumore on WVOK, the "*MIGHTY 690*" radio station in Birmingham. As a matter of fact, he became a part of our family, as each weekday he spoke the familiar words from his radio studio, "*From our house to your house.*"

One spring when my father took my brothers and me to see an exhibition baseball game at Rickwood Field in Birmingham, I insisted that we stop long enough alongside Highway 11 so that I could walk inside the WVOK studio that aired Joe Rumore.

What a great salesman he really was! Joe Rumore could talk about Martha White self-rising flour, and I wanted to run down to the country store and pick up a sack for my mother. When he talked about Golden Eagle syrup, I had visions of Mamma's homemade biscuits with syrup running down the sides. When he spoke about Hadacol, I knew that it would be a perfect remedy for all of Uncle Calvin's aches and pains.

On one occasion, Joe Rumore announced that WVOK was going to hold a contest for a brand spanking new car from

Jim Skinner Ford. He told me and all of his other avid radio listeners that the winner would be one that could answer phones correctly. My junior high girlfriend, Bunda Oliver, must have thought I was crazy when I answered the phone, "*Joe Rumore,*" instead of saying, "*Hello.*"

Joe Rumore died several years ago. When I first learned the sad news, I thought of how much I had missed him over the years and how things had changed. Joe Rumore would never have considered bashing the President of the United States. He would not have been a part of promoting racial disharmony. He would never have used the airways to attack individuals. In sharp contrast, he always talked about the good in other people. He must have loved God's great outdoors, for he often described robins nesting outside his home, and tomato plants growing in his garden. He talked about all the good things happening within our state. He encouraged people to support their schools and churches. Whenever a gospel singer would be passing through town, Joe Rumore invited him or her to the studio to sing. There was never a word of profanity spoken from the lips of Joe Rumore over the airwaves. When his Friday programs were over, people felt encouraged to go to church on Sunday.

Joe Rumore, I really miss you!

A Boyhood Memory

One of my favorite towns in Alabama is Aliceville. My maternal grandfather, John Bell, lived all of his ninety-two years in Aliceville. He was born in the front bedroom of the very home in which he died. My mother, Elizabeth Bell, was born and reared in Aliceville, and my aunt, Thelma Bell McKee, taught the third grade at the Aliceville Elementary School for more than twenty-five years.

Aliceville became a well-known town in Alabama during World War II. While our American soldiers that Tom Brokaw described as a part of "*The Greatest Generation*" were serving far away from home, seeking to stop Hitler as he made his way across Europe, a German prisoner-of-war camp was built in Aliceville. Camp Aliceville was the largest POW camp in Alabama during World War II, with 6,150 prisoners. The first prisoners arrived at the camp on June 2, 1943.

They were brought to Aliceville on trains, one of which was the old "A T and N" (Alabama, Tennessee, and Northern) Railroad that ran behind our home. My three brothers and I would sometimes walk down to the back of our pasture to watch the trains loaded with prisoners as they made their way thirty miles north of our home place. I recall seeing one of the trains blocking Highway 17 in Aliceville where the German prisoners were unloaded and moved to the prison, south of town. Many

16

of them were from Rommel's Afrika Korps, and some of them appeared to be no more than sixteen years of age. Among those German soldiers were artists, sculptors, writers, and musicians.

The German prisoners could participate in something like a *"work release"* program in the timberlands of west Alabama. My father owned a truck that transported pulpwood, and I got to know several of the prisoners. My brother Joe said that one of the German prisoners served as my babysitter.

World War II raged. Telegrams were delivered, bringing the sad news to our small community that two of my uncles had been critically wounded in battle. When World War II finally came to an end, the Aliceville POW Camp was deactivated on September 30, 1945. My uncles came back home to spend months in a stateside hospital recovering from their critical wounds. Others paid the supreme sacrifice and did not make it home.

Following World War II, I became keenly aware as a small child what Steven Ambrose calls *"the waste of war."* I know now why the great prophet Isaiah dreamed of the day when "... *They will beat their swords into plowshares and their spears into pruning hooks. Nation will not take up sword against nation, nor will they train for war anymore."* (Isaiah 2:4) While wars and rumors of wars rage all around us, perhaps our song should be, *"Let there be peace on earth and let it begin with me."*

17

A Summer Memory

I recently rode over to York, Alabama, to visit my mother. After our time together, I decided that I would drive from York up to Birmingham and visit one of our members in the hospital there. Instead of driving up Interstate 59, I chose to take old Highway 11 and relive a lot of fond memories that were a part of my youth.

I drove through Livingston where I finished high school, and there were so many wonderful memories that flooded my soul. As I continued through Epes, I saw the old baseball diamond where Brother Oliver and I once competed. I recalled a hot summer day long ago when Marcus McLelland and I skied not too far from the river bridge. When I drove north of Eutaw, I remembered the site of the old Cotton Patch Restaurant where we often dined on Saturday nights.

Driving through Tuscaloosa, I passed the First United Methodist Church that I attended when I was a student at the University of Alabama. As I passed in front of the old WVOK radio station on the north side of Bessemer, I could almost hear the voice of the late Joe Rumore selling his Hadacol and Golden Eagle syrup. As I continued on Highway 11 into Birmingham, I passed the familiar landmarks of the Alabama State Fairgrounds and Rickwood Field. When I gazed to the west, I could see the lights of Legion Field.

However, there was one place along the route of old Highway 11 that brought back a very special summer memory. It was in the little community of Knoxville, Alabama. There once stood an old country store on the east side of the highway in Knoxville. I recalled that one hot July summer afternoon long ago, my father and I stopped there and he bought a soft drink for me. When I walked out of the store, I fell down and broke my bottle on a rock. Money did not come easily in those days, and I knew deep down inside that I had wasted my father's hard-earned money.

Just when I felt the very worst, I experienced the very best. An elderly man, sitting on a nail keg in front of that country store, walked over to where I was, put his arm around me, handed me a dime, and told me to go back into the store and buy another drink.

Somehow with the passing of years, I have forgotten so many wonderful things that I experienced as a youth riding up and down Highway 11. But I have never forgotten that elderly gentleman and his simple act of kindness.

I stopped at the site of that old country store in Knoxville, Alabama, the other day. As I stood at the spot of that sacred summer memory, I offered a prayer of thanksgiving. The very same thought came to me that came to a man named Jacob long ago, "... *'Surely the Lord is in this place, and I was not aware of it.'*" (Genesis 28:16)

Being Something "Extra"

When I was a little boy, one of my greatest loves was fishing. I loved to fish in the lakes, rivers, and streams near our home in Sumter County. My uncle, John Bell, owned the Home and Auto Supply Store in York, Alabama, and one of the most exciting moments in my boyhood days came when my parents would take me to his store and let me pick out a fishing lure from his large selection of fishing tackle. I can still visualize those fishing lures hanging on the south wall of his store, and I can recall how I would stand there for the longest period of time before making a final decision.

After I had made my choice and paid for the lure, Uncle John would place it in a brown paper bag, and I would begin the seventeen-mile trip back home with my parents. When I got home and opened the bag, I always discovered to my pleasant surprise that Uncle John had "thrown in" an extra lure for good measure.

There is a wonderful practice in certain parts of Louisiana called "lagniappe." When someone goes to a store and buys a dozen items, it is not uncommon for that person to get back home and find an "extra" item thrown in.

Jesus, in the Sermon on the Mount, asked His disciples, ". . . w*hat are you doing more than others?"* (Matthew 5:47) Jesus talked about doing the "extra" things in life. He talked about going the second mile, turning the other cheek, and forgiving seventy times seven. In other words, He expected His followers to be something "extra" in all of their relationships in life.

It was Bishop Robert Goodrich who phrased the question years ago, "*If you were arrested for being a Christian, would there be enough evidence to convict you?*" Perhaps that is the question that all of us need to ponder as we make our pilgrimages through life. Let us be willing to do the "extra" in the spirit of Jesus Christ.

My Most Memorable Christmas

Christmas is filled with nostalgia, and all of us have wonderful memories of very special Christmas celebrations of bygone years. As I reflect upon all of the unforgettable experiences of celebrating Christmas in the past, there is one that seems to stand out above all of the rest. It took place on Christmas Eve when I was a teenager.

My father owned a service station beside Highway 17 over in Sumter County in the small community of Emelle. Within that service station, he sold candy, cookies, and other snacks. On that particular Christmas Eve as I was helping my father, I was thinking only of closing time and the Christmas gifts I might receive the following morning. It was then that my father taught me one of the most valuable lessons of my life. He said, *"Son, if you are thinking only of yourself tonight and all of the things that you might receive for Christmas, this Christmas will soon fade into a distant memory. However, if you will load up some of these snacks and take them to a poor family not far from here, this Christmas will remain in your memory for a lifetime."*

I was somewhat reluctant to follow my father's advice, wondering how the poor family might respond. However, I filled several large (Number 12) brown paper bags with peppermint sticks, orange slices, chocolate covered cherries, chewing gum, and other items. I drove my father's jeep to the poor family's home just across the Mississippi line, approximately four miles west of where we lived. When I knocked on the door of their modest wood frame house, the family members warmly welcomed me and invited me in. There was not a single reminder within their whole house that Christmas was near. There were no Christmas trees, no lights, no ornaments, no greenery, no candles, no holly, and no mistletoe. Needless to say there were no gifts.

However, as I entered that home that night and gave to the wide-eyed children the contents of those brown paper bags, joy and excitement filled their faces. As I turned around and drove back home that cold winter evening, there was a warm feeling within my heart like I had never felt before. Suddenly, it dawned upon me the significant truth of the only words of Jesus that are recorded in the Book of Acts (20:35), ". . . *'It is more blessed to give than to receive.'"*

So many wonderful memories of Christmas celebrations have truly faded into the distant past, but the one Christmas that I was encouraged by my father to do something for someone less fortunate will remain in my memory forever.

Only a Mother's Love

When my mother's health began to fail and it became necessary for her to move into a nursing home, I went back to our old home place to pick up some items that were precious to me as a child. While I was there, I noticed the old cedar chest that had occupied a prominent place in my mother's bedroom. When I lifted up the top of that cedar chest, I could hardly believe my eyes. There in that cedar chest, my mother had not only saved, but neatly stacked, every single church newsletter that I had sent to her from every church that I served from the very first day I entered the ministry. She had even gone to great lengths to organize them according to months and years. She had taken pieces of worn string and made a bundle for each year. Each newsletter that I had sent to her across the past thirty-six years was placed in proper chronological order. There in that cedar chest were weekly newsletters and articles that I had written while I served in Andalusia, Alabama; Bonifay, Florida; Whitfield Memorial in Montgomery, Alabama; Troy, Alabama; and all of my years at First United Methodist Church in Montgomery.

Needless to say, there were so many of those newsletters with my articles on the front that no one would want to keep. Some of my front page articles had been written to promote special events or programs that had been planned for the respective churches that I served. Others were written to welcome guest speakers. There were many articles that were anything but inspirational.

However, as I picked up each bundle of newsletters, I must confess that I was overcome with emotion. All of a sudden it struck me that it was not the quality of the front page articles that caused my mother to save each newsletter. No, I was wise enough to realize in that moment that it was simply that I was her son, and she was my mother, and that special relationship overshadowed the content of the pages I had written. For those who do not know my mother, you would be interested to know that she was reared in a culture where it did not come natural for people to say, "*I love you.*" Yet, down through the years, her sacrificial love for my brothers and me has been evident in so many simple deeds.

When I brought those bundles of newsletters back home to Montgomery, I was reminded once again that a mother's love, next to God's love, has to be the most wonderful love in all of the world. I was also reminded that a mother's love always expresses itself in the simple things of life — a word of encouragement, a telephone call, a listening ear, a sympathizing tear, and yes, even worn strings that hold together thirty-six years of newsletters.

Making Our Way
Back Home

Several years ago, my family and I were invited to be the guests of Brenda's parents on a trip to Alaska. It was a marvelous experience visiting the "Land of the Midnight Sun." I was captivated by the beautiful scenery and the awe inspiring glaciers, but the one thing that caught my attention the most was the salmon. We were there during the month of August and saw the salmon in the midst of their spawning season.

Salmon are hatched in the freshwater streams. Scientists claim that these salmon swim as far as two thousand miles out into the Pacific Ocean. Amazingly enough, the salmon somehow have the ability to return to within a few feet of the place where they were hatched.

Some scientists claim that the salmon sense the magnetic field of the earth and the currents of the ocean. After reaching the coast, the salmon apparently remember the odor of their home stream and follow that scent. All I know is that the salmon, driven by one of the strongest instincts in nature, find their way back across the trackless Pacific Ocean, elude fishermen, battle upriver, leap ten feet high waterfalls and man-made obstructions to get back "home."

There are so many mysteries of life that we can never explain. Yet, God has implanted within each of us the amazing ability to discern His will and way. Sometimes we might wander far away from home. Sometimes we might lose our course or sense of direction. Yet, God has given us the innate ability to discern when we are on track and moving in the direction He would have us go. When our lives are lived in harmony with His will, there is a sense of peace and contentment that causes us to know that we are "at home again" with the Lord.

One of my favorite verses of scripture is Isaiah 26:3, *"You will keep in perfect peace him whose mind is steadfast, because he trusts in you."*

My Favorite Cat Story

When my family and I previously lived in Montgomery (1974-80), we lived at 2519 Gladlane Drive, just off McGehee Road. Our younger daughter, Carmen, was six months old when we moved there and six years old when we moved away.

While we were living there on Gladlane Drive, a military family two blocks away had a cat named Marble. The cat became closely attached to Carmen who gave her much attention. The cat practically lived at our back door. Even though the military family would often come and pick her up, the cat would always come back.

Once the cat had a litter of six kittens at our back door. The military family came over to our home, placed all of the newborn kittens in a basket, and took them back to their home. However, Marble brought them back, one by one, to our rear door.

When the military family moved away, they gave the cat to Carmen because the two of them had become so attached. Soon afterwards, we moved to Troy and lived there for three-and-a-half years. We then moved back to Montgomery to live on Aimee Drive, located in Vaughn Meadows. Shortly after we moved in, we went out of town to enjoy Thanksgiving dinner with my in-laws. When we returned Thanksgiving night to our new residence in Montgomery, our cat was gone. We searched far and wide for the cat, but it was to no avail. We placed advertisements about our lost cat in the local newspaper, as well as on the radio. We even drove back down toward Troy to see if our cat might be walking alongside Highway 231 in an effort to go back to our former home there.

Several months passed. One day, Brenda decided to go see our former neighbor, Grace Sanders, on Gladlane Drive. As they shared old times together, Brenda asked if she had seen our cat. Grace said, *"No, but our neighbors told me that a cat has been around here since Thanksgiving."*

To sum it up, we had moved from Montgomery to Troy, back to a new home in Montgomery, and our cat left the first day back in Montgomery and went back to our first Montgomery home.

We marvel at all of God's creatures as they long to go back home to a place of security. God has placed within each of our hearts a yearning to be in His eternal presence. We can identify with those words of St. Augustine, *"O Lord, thou has made us for thyself, and our hearts are restless until they find rest in Thee."*

Family Vacation (?) at Disney World

Brenda and I had looked forward for many weeks to taking our two precious grandchildren, Hannah and Mary Carmen, to Disney World. Stacie and Kevin had left no stone unturned in organizing this wonderful family vacation. When I learned that our first day there would be spent at the Animal Kingdom, I grew even more excited, anticipating the viewing of different species. However, I quickly learned that the most interesting part of the trip would be that of observing the human species!

We arrived at the Animal Kingdom at 10:30 a.m. There was not a cloud in the sky! The bright sunshine warmly greeted us, along with tens of thousands of other people who rushed through the gates. I was just inside the entrance when I observed a wife with her hands on her hips screaming at her husband, "*I told you to meet me here at 10:00 a.m.! I knew that you would be late! You always get lost!*" A little further into the park, I overheard a man yelling at his wife, "*Where is the camera? The last thing I told you was not to forget the camera!*"

As noon drew near, the sun overhead was getting hotter and hotter. I was tempted to ask that old question, "*Are we having fun yet?*" It was then that I decided to wait in the 65-minute line for the African Safari. As I stood in line, I noticed that the woman just in front of me had a large tattoo (spider) that glistened from her heavy perspiration. All around me by now, I could hear a myriad of children's voices screaming, "*I want a Coke... The seat in the stroller is too hot... Someone stepped on my foot... I want an autograph book for all of the Disney characters... I want my Mama!*"

The sun had reached its zenith by 2:00 p.m. The rising temperature was accompanied by rising tempers all around me. I had learned by now that the coolest places at Disney World were the rides, so I decided to take in as many rides as possible. I rode the Space Mountain Roller Coaster, Goofy's Family Roller Coaster, Mad Tea Party Spin Around, and a Race Car on the Indy Speedway.

By 3:00 p.m., my head was swooning from all of the rides. Amid my dizzy spells, I could faintly hear beautiful music in the far distance coming from Cinderella's Castle. However, the most beautiful music to my ears was the sound of my younger granddaughter, Mary Carmen, who said, "*Papa, I've had enough! I want to go home!*" As we slowly dragged our tired bodies back to our hotel, I was reminded that the day's activities reflected so much of life. All of us at one time or another feel the heated pressures of life bearing down upon us. When heated pressures come our way, we need to remember those words that the Apostle Paul wrote to the Romans, "*Do not conform any longer to the pattern of this world . . . .*" (Romans 12:2) **I am now trying to work into my busy schedule a vacation to get over our most recent family vacation (?) to Disney World!**

31

Congratulations, Graduates!

Our younger daughter, Carmen, graduates from Jefferson Davis High School this Friday night. It is hard to believe that time moves so swiftly. It seems like only yesterday when Carmen was born at Southeast Alabama General Hospital in Dothan, Alabama. We were living in Bonifay, Florida, at the time, and we drove the thirty-seven miles to Dothan in the middle of the night for this exciting birth to take place.

There have been so many wonderful moments along the way — school plays, cheerleading, ballet, state spelling bee, confirmation, youth choir tours, science fairs, driver's license, fashion shows, family vacations, and now graduation.

There have been a few bumps and bruises along the way — a broken arm, a minor car accident — but for most of the journey, it has been a wonderful experience for us.

One unforgettable moment was when Carmen was learning how to drive in preparation for her driver's exam. She was sitting alone in our car in the driveway, driving it forward and backward a few feet when the motor went dead. The car began to roll out of the driveway, and she could not get the brakes to work without the engine running. She jumped out of the car, and I later found it against the tree across the street in our neighbor's yard. God has surely protected us through all of these years!

As we celebrate this week with so many other parents whose children are also graduating from high school, I wanted to share with you a quotation that some unknown parent shared with his child on graduation day.

It's Your Move!

I gave you life, but I cannot live it for you.
I can teach you things, but I cannot make you learn.
I can give you directions,
but I cannot always be there to lead you.
I can teach you right from wrong,
but I cannot always decide for you.
I can offer you advice, but I cannot accept it for you.
I can teach you to be a friend, but I cannot make you one.
I can teach you to share, but I cannot make you unselfish.
I can teach you respect, but I cannot force you to show honor.
I can warn you about drugs,
but I cannot prevent you from using them.
I can warn you about the consequences of sin,
but I cannot make your morals.
I can pray for you, but I cannot make you walk with God.
I can tell you how to live, but I cannot give you eternal life.

A New Resident at Our Home!

Brenda and I have welcomed a new "resident" to our home. It is a beautiful killdeer that is nesting four eggs on top of some pine straw in our front yard. Our new "resident" is so typical of all killdeers — eight inches in length, thick dark bill, flesh-colored legs, red eye rings, white forehead and white stripe behind eyes, brown face, white collar, and two black breast bands on her white breast. As she sits continually on her nest during this 24-28 day incubation period, I notice when I leave home early in the morning that her mate serves her "breakfast in bed" with assorted worms and other choice food items! Whenever I walk near the nesting killdeer, she ruffles her feathers like a setting hen. She is so protective of her eggs that I can literally walk within inches of her before she is willing to move off her nest. In those rare moments when she does move off her nest, I am amazed how the little killdeer's nest and four little eggs blend marvelously into the background.

The killdeer is named for its loud cry which can sound like "kill-deer." One of the most fascinating things to me is that the killdeer is one of many shorebirds that performs the "crippled bird act" if their nests or young are threatened. The bird calls rapidly, drags one or both wings pitifully on the ground, spreads its tail, and even limps to one side to distract the intruder. When the intruder has left the area, the bird is "healed" and flies away!

Our new resident has reaffirmed for me, not only the wonder of God's creation, but also our need to be more caring of all of God's creatures. After all, Jesus said, "*Look at the birds of the air....*" (Matthew 6:26)

John L. Gwartney wrote the following lines long ago in appreciation of a farmer who was sensitive to killdeers in his midst.

> Oh bless the man who finds the time,
> While working with his plow,
> To pass the little killdeer's nest,
> And make it safe somehow.
> 'Twas God who made both bird and man,
> We know not why nor how,
> The one he made to nest the fields,
> The other one to plow.
> And as she flutters from her nest,
> To lead you far astray,
> 'Twas He who put the instinct there
> To save her nest this day.
> Since He saw fit to put her there,
> To make the fields less bare,
> Let's do our best to help preserve,
> The things left in our care!

For All Dads!

The late Judge Joe Phelps was a personal friend of mine who had such a positive influence upon our city. On the Sunday morning prior to his tragic automobile accident, he spoke at the Men's Club at First United Methodist Church of Montgomery. On that occasion, he spoke of the great importance of the love of a father for a child. He shared, in closing, a quotation that I wanted to pass along to all fathers.

When they got scared, it was your hand they clutched. When they couldn't see the parade, it was your shoulders they sat on. When they wanted an ice cream cone, it was your pocket they tugged. When they scratched their knee, it was your lap they cried in.

When they built a house of blocks, they sought out your approval. When the neighbors' kids didn't treat them right, it was your hug they wanted. When they struck out at the baseball game, it was your eyes they tried to avoid. When they learned the new trick on the bike, it was you they wanted to impress.

When they received honors at school, you were the first to see the trophy. When they met the perfect girl or guy, you were the important one to get introduced. When they got the promotion at work, you were the first person they called.

The reason's simple. You're their daddy — you always have been and always will be.

Daddy is the one who finds the way to tell his children, no matter what they do, no matter where they go, no matter how long it's been, no matter how old they are, no matter what it costs —

> If I have a penny, you'll never be broke.
> If I have a loaf of bread, you won't go hungry.
> If I have a shirt, you won't be cold.
> If I have an arm, you'll always be hugged.

And if I don't have a penny, or a loaf of bread, or a shirt, or enough power in my tired arms to hug anymore, come stand by my bed and hold my hand, and know that if there's a heart left in this old body, then Daddy still loves you.

Thinking of Brenda, "The Wind Beneath My Wings"

Brenda and I are preparing to celebrate our fortieth wedding anniversary this Sunday, August 28, 2005, and that is the reason that I have been thinking about her so much this week, as well as the lyrics to Bette Midler's popular song, "The Wind Beneath My Wings."

It must have been cold there in my shadow,
to never have sunlight on your face.
You were content to let me shine, that's your way,
you always walked a step behind.
So I was the one with all the glory,
while you were the one with all the strength.
A beautiful face without a name—
for so long, a beautiful smile to hide the pain.
It might have appeared to go unnoticed,
but I've got it all here in my heart.
I want you to know I know the truth.
Of course, I know it. I would be nothing without you!
Did you ever know that you're my hero,
And ev'rything I would like to be?
I can fly higher than an eagle,

'cause you are the wind beneath my wings.

It seems only yesterday on a hot August afternoon that Brenda, as a beautiful bride, walked down the aisle of the Flomaton Methodist Church, and we were married. What a great source of strength and inspiration she has been to me across these past forty years! It takes a very special person to be a minister's wife. A minister's wife is always living in a fishbowl! She is expected to move on a moment's notice, live in someone else's home, and worry about meeting other people's unfair expectations. However, one of the things that I have admired so much about Brenda down through the years has been her simple desire to be her own best self. She is truly one of the most genuine persons that I have ever known. She has never sought the spotlight. She has never sought to be the "first lady" of the church. She has never wanted to preach. She has never asked to direct the choir. She has never even wanted to sit on the front pew. She has always preferred to sit among our members at the rear of the sanctuary.

Brenda is truly one of those *always* people, who is *always* there to support and encourage me, as she *always* supports the church. She just goes about doing good, working mostly behind the scenes in a thousand different ways to touch the lives of others. Across the years, she has taught elementary Sunday School classes, directed children's choirs, delivered meals to the elderly, participated in the United Methodist Women, and worked on the bazaar. Wherever we have served together, she has been the one that everyone dearly loved, and she has made every appointment for us very, very special!

Her role as a mother has been fantastic! God blessed us with two wonderful daughters, Stacie and Carmen. Brenda has *always* been there for them every step of the way. When God blessed us with three grandchildren, Hannah, Mary Carmen, and Karlson, Brenda's role as a grandmother became even more admirable. Yes, there have been so many family vacations that were cut short because of unexpected happenings at the church. There have been so many church events that have taken precedence over planned activities with the children. However, Brenda has always been so understanding and never complained when my role as a minister interfered with our family activities.

There is a great verse of scripture found in Proverbs 31:10-11, *"A wife of noble character who can find? She is worth far more than rubies. Her husband has full confidence in her and lacks nothing of value."* That's Brenda, and I just wanted her to know how much I love her, and thank her for *always* being there across these past forty years!

I Don't Remember Anymore

I love the story of the two little boys who enrolled in first grade of elementary school. On the first day of school, the teacher asked the two little brothers about their *birthdays*. The first little brother said, "I was born on January 1, 2000." The second said, "I was born on April 4, 2000." The teacher smiled and asked, "How could it be that you were born so close together?"

One of the little brothers spoke up and said, "One of us is adopted." The teacher knelt down before both of them and said, "Which of you is adopted?"

One little boy said, "I asked my daddy one day, 'Which one of us is adopted?' and my daddy knelt down and gave us both a big hug and kiss and said, 'I don't remember anymore.'" Paul writes in Romans 8:17, "*Now if we are children, then we are heirs— heirs of God and co-heirs with Christ. . . .*"

Of all the billions of persons on the face of the earth, I feel it utterly amazing that each individual has a unique set of fingerprints. Surely God continues to remind us that each of us is a unique part of his creation. "Mister Rogers" reminded the children of his television audience each day, "I think you are special, and I like you just the way you are." Let us remember that, that each of us is very special in the eyes of God.

The Church in Your Home

Dr. Willis Tate served for a number of years as President of Southern Methodist University in Dallas, Texas. He told the delightful story of one day receiving a letter from a mother in rural west Texas whose son was enrolling for his freshman year at SMU. The mother was anxious that her son get off to a good start in college, and so she had written Dr. Tate, asking if he might intercede on her behalf to find a good roommate for her son. According to Dr. Tate, the mother had requested in her letter that he find her son a roommate who was a good student so that her son might develop good student habits. She wanted a roommate for her son who did not use foul language, for she did not want her son picking up any words of profanity. She also wanted her son to have a roommate who was not interested in girls, because she did not want any girls distracting his attention from studies or leading him astray. When this dear mother came to the close of her letter, she added a P.S., " The reason that I am writing this letter to you is simply because this is the first time that my son has been away from home except for the four years that he spent in the United States Marine Corps."

I am sure that all of you would agree with me that the dear mother out in rural Texas was somewhat naïve. Yet, oftentimes, I feel as though we parents are equally naïve in our expectations of schools and churches. We live in a world where

42

we tend to compartmentalize life. We think of the school as the place where our children will receive their education. We think of the church as the place where our children will receive their religious training. Yet, more education or religious training is taught, or perhaps "caught," in the home than is ever taught or "caught" in our schools and churches.

There is a very interesting phrase that is found in the letters of Paul. He writes, *"... and to the church that meets in your home ...."* (Philemon 2) The early Christians met in homes to sing, to pray, and to study God's word. They had no beautiful sanctuaries like we enjoy today. Yet the fascinating phrase *"... and to the church that meets in your home ..."* is so true to life. More basic theology is communicated within the home than could ever be taught by all of the seminary professors of the world. Perhaps all of us would be wise to pause and ask ourselves the question, "What lessons about God, Jesus Christ, and the church are we teaching in our homes?"

My Heart is Hurting Today

Brenda and I are joining so many other parents this week who are watching their first child go off to college. It seems only yesterday when Dr. Gary Cumbie walked out of the waiting room at the Andalusia Hospital with a big broad smile and said to me, "It's a girl!" Stacie leaves this week for college, and I know that the next few days will be days of great adjustment for my family and me. Brenda and I will be reminded that when we as parents have done all that we can, we must leave the results to God. There must come a time when all parents must be willing to "Let go and let God." In light of this, I was deeply touched the other day when I read the words of another father who watched his child go off to college.

> My heart is hurting today. I took Cindy to college yesterday. My wife and I loaded all of our daughter's things into the van and drove all the way to Bloomington, Indiana, where Cindy is enrolling as a freshman at the University of Indiana. The time to say 'good-bye' came too quickly. I have a different soft-spot for each of my children, and I got so emotional when I hugged Cindy that I was embarrassed when those other parents walked by. I quickly hopped behind the wheel of the van, waved good-bye and drove off. I will never forget looking back at that girl, standing so alone in front of that big dormitory, holding back tears of her own and

waving good-bye — not only to my wife and me, but to a past chapter of her life and ours that we will never know again.

I couldn't talk for the first twenty miles. It was all I could do to keep from turning around and going back to get her. There were so many things that I still wanted to tell her. It was as if I were molding something in my hands and someone took it out of my hands before I was done with it. Finally, when my voice came back, I told my wife how I felt, and she rightly pointed out that you never really finish a child. 'That is up to Cindy to do,' she said. 'We must sort of put the clay together, and now it is up to her to shape the final mold.'

That is a valuable lesson that all of us parents need to learn. We parents never really finish a child. We merely put the clay together and pray that somewhere, somehow, someone along life's way will help us shape the final mold.

Thank You, God, for a Wonderful Mother!

How can I say thanks to God for such a wonderful mother! Because of the goodness of God within her life, I have been so richly blessed. When my phone rang at six o'clock this morning, bringing me the news that my 97-year-old mother had died, I must confess that the news did not come as a great surprise. However, I was surprised by the deep sense of emotion that welled up within my heart. All mothers are very, very special, and so it was in the case of my mother. It was my dear mother who brought me into this world, who experienced my first heartbeat, and witnessed my first breath. She was one of those *always* people, those rare individuals who have always been there and somehow you begin to believe that they will always be there.

In the eyes of other people, my mother was known for several distinguished roles in her life — teacher, clerk, historian. However, for me she was simply my mother. She was my life-bringer, nurturer, encourager, affirmer, supporter, adviser, sympathizer, and consoler. Like all other mothers, she had experienced her share of joys and sorrows of life. I saw her lose a child in a tragic accident, but she never lost her faith in the love and goodness of God.

There was not a lot of hugging and kissing around our home, yet my mother expressed her love to me in a million different ways. There was no job too menial for my mother to do as she sought to provide for five sons. As a little boy, I observed that my mother was going to make whatever sacrifices necessary in order that each of us might have an opportunity to get a college education. Yet, all of my college and seminary courses put together could not compare with what my mother did to teach me about Jesus Christ and the church.

My mother had a very simple, but strict philosophy of life, *"Honor God. Study the Bible. Follow the teachings of Jesus. Go to church on Sunday. Serve your fellowman. Work hard. Get a good education. Read good books. Be honest. Always say 'Yes, Sir' and 'No, Sir' to your elders. Don't ever forget to say 'Thank you.' Mind your own business. Don't get too big for your britches. Help those who are less fortunate. Take care of your life, and God will take care of your death!"*

Amazingly enough, I can still hear my Mother's voice! With a heart that overflows with gratitude for my mother who died this morning, I just wanted to say, *"Thank you, God, for a wonderful Mother!"*

Chapter Two

Memories of Church

I Stopped to Help Her Cry!

Several years ago, the editor of the *United Methodist Reporter* out in Dallas, Texas, invited subscribers of this fine church publication to submit stories that they had heard in church that had lingered in their minds. I was curiously interested in the very first story that was printed.

An elderly lady in Los Osos, California, submitted a story that she had heard in church as a child and had never forgotten. Her minister had told the story of a mother who had sent her young daughter down the street to pick up a loaf of bread. The little girl was late returning home. The mother grew very anxious. When the little girl walked through the door, the mother asked, "Where have you been?"

Her daughter replied, "I came across my friend from down the street who had broken her doll."

"Oh," the mother responded, "and you stopped to help her fix it."

"No," the little girl replied, "I stopped to help her cry."

The elderly lady who remembered that story throughout her long life had done so simply because it is so true to our human experience. When persons we love experience some tragedy within their lives — a child killed, a tragic accident, a loss of a job — it is impossible within our human vocabularies to express our deepest feelings of love and support. Yet during the midst of those difficult times we must remember that we are not called to *say the right words.* We are simply called to be a ministry of presence that can make a significant difference.

The Apostle Paul, in that magnificent twelfth chapter of Romans, reminded us, *"Rejoice with those who rejoice, mourn with those who mourn."* (Romans 12:15)

My Most
Unforgettable Wedding!

I love weddings! Having officiated at over 1,000 weddings, I have never had a bride or groom who could not participate because of illness. Doesn't that say something about the amazing power of love?

My most unforgettable wedding took place when I was pastor of the First United Methodist Church in Bonifay, Florida. A wonderful young couple in that county seat town planned a big Saturday night wedding. On the night of the wedding, family members and friends overflowed the sanctuary. When the wedding ceremony had ended and I was hanging up my robe in my office, the best man handed me the marriage license. I was stunned when I read at the top of the license, "Houston County, Alabama." I immediately called a circuit judge who was a member of our church and asked, "Can you marry a couple in Florida with an Alabama marriage license?"

He responded "No! You need to drive the couple across the Alabama state line and have another wedding ceremony." I called my minister friends just across the Florida-Alabama state line in places like Hartford, Geneva, Samson to see if I could use one of their churches. Of course, no one was at home on that Saturday night.

51

When the wedding reception had ended, the young couple came by my office. I said, "I regret to tell you that you are not married. You cannot get married in Florida with an Alabama marriage license. We need to drive up into Alabama and do this again to make it legal."

I got into my car with the bride and groom in the back seat. We drove north on Highway 79 until we crossed the Alabama state line. I spotted a giant cedar tree on the west side of the road (Alabama Highway 167) and drove underneath it. The groom, dressed in his tuxedo, got out of the car and opened the door for his bride in her long, flowing bridal gown and train. As they stood under that cedar tree, I began to lead them in their vows. Cars filled with teenagers headed south to Panama City blew their horns loudly. Drivers of other cars slammed on their brakes to check out this moonlight wedding.

I passed that large cedar tree the other day and I could not help but smile. I wondered what happened to that couple. Did they have children? Did they realize that when a bride and groom pledge their love to one another, even underneath a giant cedar tree, that site becomes sacred ground? I wondered if they had remembered their vows, *"for better, for worse, for richer, for poorer, in sickness and in health, 'till death do us part."* I also wondered if they still laugh about their wedding under the light of the silvery moon!

A Doxology That Became a Wedding March

While vacationing at Pensacola Beach several summers ago, I had the privilege of worshiping at the wonderful Gulf Breeze United Methodist Church. Dr. Paul A. Nixon, the associate pastor, preached a splendid sermon, and I found their patriotic service on that Sunday following Independence Day to be very inspiring.

However, there was one unforgettable experience that transpired at the 8:30 a.m. service. It occurred following the offering where the people normally stand and sing as the organist plays the doxology. Their organ is programmed in such a way that one can simply push a button and the doxology can be played even without the organist present.

As you can imagine, someone had changed the stops on the organ the previous evening, and the organ played "The Wedding March" as the two ushers walked down the aisle side by side with the offering plates. As the congregation broke out in laughter and the music ceased, one of the ushers proudly exclaimed, "*I do!*"

Robert Burns reminded us long ago, "The best laid plans of mice and men often go astray." This is true, not only in churches, but also within our individual lives. We live in an imperfect world as imperfect people.

Whenever our best laid plans go astray, we need to be reminded that God has always used imperfect people like ourselves to accomplish great things for Him. Jesus even used a blundering fisherman named Simon Peter to be the Prince of the Apostles. The good news is that God can even redeem our imperfect doxologies and use each of us in ceaseless praise!

Jack's Seat

Brenda and I were married in the Flomaton United Methodist Church on August 28, 1965. It is a pretty little church with lots of wonderful people, and down through the years, I have grown to appreciate the faithfulness of that congregation.

One of the most faithful members of the Flomaton United Methodist Church was Jack McCloud. Although he was not endowed with all of the mental faculties that most people enjoy, Jack was still smart enough to make his way to church Sunday after Sunday. As a matter of fact, he was always there before the doors opened.

Shortly before Brenda and I were married, I walked into her home church to visit one Sunday morning. After the usher greeted me warmly and handed me a bulletin, I walked over to the side aisle on the left and took my seat at the end of the back pew. I had been sitting there only a few minutes listening to the prelude when there was a tap on my left shoulder. I turned around and it was Jack. He looked at me very seriously and said, "*You have my seat!*" I moved over and let Jack sit down in the place where he sat Sunday after Sunday.

I laughed about that incident when it happened, but down through the years, I have grown to love and appreciate persons like Jack who are so regular in their worship attendance Sunday after Sunday that they almost claim a seat of their own in church. All of us are creatures of habit, even when it comes to church attendance and the very seats that we choose.

A sanctuary has always been viewed as a "place of refuge," a place where we can leave behind all of the burdens of life and in the presence of God experience that *"peace which passeth all understanding."* I give thanks to God for persons like Jack who claim the same pew Sunday after Sunday!

Jesus Came from the Wrong Direction!

There was something very amusing that happened at our church on Palm Sunday that most of our 3,600 members never realized. Our children had gathered on the front of the lawn of the church for the annual reenactment of the Palm Sunday story. The weather was perfect, the crowd was great, the narrator was wonderful, and all of the children had been given their palm branches to wave as Jesus, riding on a donkey, made his triumphant entry. Our fifth graders had been placed on the south part of the lawn to lay branches in the path of Jesus as He made His royal processional into the Holy City!

However, there was one major thing that did not go according to plan. The planned script as prepared by Glenda Argo, our splendid Children's Director, had Jesus entering from the south. Lo and behold, much to her surprise and the surprise of others who had a part in planning the event, Jesus came from the north riding on the donkey.

There were very few people in the audience that even realized what had happened. However, as I laughed about the event, I could not help but think there must be a message in all of this.

The Jesus portrayed in the gospels is one who is always full of surprises. The great surprise of His birth is that it did not happen in Athens, Rome, or Cairo but rather in Bethlehem on the backside of nowhere. It did not happen beneath a golden dome, but rather in a lowly stable. The news of His birth did not come from someone aboard Air Force One surrounded by powerful dignitaries. No, His birth was first made known to lowly shepherds out in the fields. When you look at the earthly ministry of Jesus, you also discover that His ministry was full of surprises. He accepted those whom society rejected, and He rejected those whom society had accepted. If Jesus had chosen to live only among the righteous, what a lonely life He would have lived upon this earth. In sharp contrast to what we might have expected, Jesus reached out to the least, the last, and the lost.

Whenever we are tempted to put Jesus "in a box," just remember that He is always full of surprises!

Adams Hudson's Cowboy

Adams Hudson, our artist-in-residence, designed the beautiful stone carvings that are found over the doors of our new Wesley Hall. When the carvings arrived from Indiana, it was evident that our stonemason was not overly familiar with Methodist history. He simply informed me that the *"cowboy"* had arrived. When I walked outside to see what he was talking about, I was pleasantly surprised to see Adams' rendition of John Wesley on horseback!

As United Methodists, we trace our heritage back to John Wesley (1703-1791). It was on Aldersgate Street on May 24, 1738, that his heart was *"strangely warmed."* With that experience came his burning desire to share the good news of Jesus Christ with everyone. It is of little surprise that John Wesley said, *"The world is my parish!"* Since Wesley was denied the opportunity to speak in many of the churches of England, even the one at Epworth where his father served for thirty-nine years, he mounted his horse and moved out into the fields. He often rode sixty to seventy miles a day, covering over 250,000 miles on horseback during his lifetime. When he was seventy-eight years of age, he wrote of traveling 280 miles in forty-eight hours. For more than fifty years, he preached an average of three times a day.

When Methodism spread to our United States, the frontier preachers were known as *"circuit riders,"* for they traveled on horseback around a circuit of churches. Dr. Harold E. Luccock wrote in *Endless Line of Splendor,* "Of the first 737 members of the Conferences to die, 203 were between 25 and 35 years of age, and 121 between 35 and 45. Nearly half of them died before they were 30 years of age. Of 675 of the first preachers whose records we have in full, two-thirds died before they were able to render 12 years of service. The majority of them burned themselves out for God in a few years."

The next time you see a stone carving on a church that depicts a man riding a horse, just remember that it is a symbol of something far greater than a cowboy. It is a symbol of John Wesley who rode over 250,000 miles on horseback to share the good news of Jesus Christ.

Faith in the Future

When George Awsumb, an architect from Memphis, Tennessee, drew the architectural plans for our beautiful sanctuary at First United Methodist Church of Montgomery nearly sixty years ago, he chose to place the stone carvings of the faces of his own two children high above the front entrance. If you stand today on the landing in front of the sanctuary and look high above, you will see the faces of a little boy and a little girl.

That "little" boy, Richard Awsumb, now a retired architect in Memphis, called me one day to tell me an interesting story. He said that when he was only seven years of age, his father took him and his sister down to the Christy Stone Company there in Memphis so that the stone carver could make models of their heads and faces to be used on the front of First United Methodist Church of Montgomery. Sixty years later, he received a telephone call from Mr. Fred Christy of the Christy Stone Company there in Memphis saying that he had something to give to him. When Richard Awsumb went down to the Christy Stone Company, he was very much surprised to hear Fred Christy say, "We want to give you a model of your face that was used when the First Methodist Church of Montgomery was built in the 1930s. We have been using it for a doorstop for over fifty years!"

Why did George Awsumb, the architect, place the faces of his two children on the front of our sanctuary? Perhaps like all proud parents he wanted to express a great love for his children. Our sanctuary was built in the midst of the Great Depression. Mr. Awsumb may have wanted to place the faces of his children on the front of our sanctuary as a simple reminder during those difficult days that he still had faith and hope in the future.

The Apostle Paul wrote to the Romans, *". . . we also rejoice in our sufferings, because we know that suffering produces perseverance; perseverance, character; and character, hope. And hope does not disappoint us, because God has poured out his love into our hearts by the Holy Spirit, whom he has given us."* (Romans 5:3-5)

Decorating the Wrong Car

Something very amusing happened following a wedding at First United Methodist Church located in beautiful Cloverdale Park of Montgomery. The groom owned a dark blue Honda Accord, and he parked his car in front of the church so that he and his lovely bride might make their "getaway" for their honeymoon.

Glenda Argo, our Director of Christian Education, had previously planned a workshop for our Sunday School teachers on that very same day of the wedding. Glenda also owned a dark blue Honda Accord, and she also parked it in front of the church.

When the Sunday School workshop had come to an end and the wedding was still in progress, Glenda walked out front to get into her car and found that her car had been decorated all over. The groomsmen had taken white shoe polish and written "Just Married" and other things all over the windows. They had tied tin cans and tissue paper streamers to the rear bumper.

When the wedding was over and the bride and groom discovered that the groomsmen had decorated the wrong car, they were embarrassed beyond words. They were very apologetic and insisted that the brother of the bride take Glenda's car for a "super car wash" at their expense.

When I reflect upon that amusing experience, I think of how often we become confused and decorate the wrong things in life. We spend an enormous amount of time and energy making sure that our children wear all of the "right" clothes. We put forth the extra effort to make sure that they have all of the cultural advantages and belong to the "right" clubs. Yet too often we forget the greater importance of "inner beauty" that comes when a child submits his or her life to the teachings of Jesus Christ.

I wonder what would happen today if we were just as concerned with our children's "inward" beauty as we are concerned with their "outward" beauty. When we put a greater emphasis on "outer beauty" than "inner beauty," we find ourselves "decorating the wrong things."

Miss Bessie

Several years ago I was invited to go back home to the Emelle Community Church and officiate at a funeral service. Going back home always evokes warm feelings of bygone years and fond memories of persons who significantly touched my life as a child. When the funeral service that day had ended, I turned to the organist, Mrs. Bessie Fuller, and whispered, "How long have you been playing the piano and organ for the church?" I was somewhat taken aback when she responded, "Seventy-six years!" "Miss Bessie" has been playing for all of the Sunday School assemblies, morning and evening worship services, revivals, weddings, and funerals for the past 2,552 Sundays. I began to wonder how many pianists/organists in the world of United Methodism have been playing for seventy-six consecutive years in the very same church. Like a giant oak of a familiar landscape, "Miss Bessie" has always been there.

There is something to be said for the faithfulness of people like "Miss Bessie." Over the past seventy-six years, surely there were those Sundays when she had out-of-town guests. Surely there were those Sundays when she woke up feeling blue. Surely there were those Sundays long ago when she had difficulty getting her four children—Sara Ann, Wren, Burton, and Howard—dressed for church. I asked her, "How many Sundays have you missed over the past seventy-six years? " She answered, "About five."

Her father, John Wesley Burton, was a local pastor who helped her realize at an early age that her musical talents were truly a gift from God and they were to be used for His glory. She began playing the piano for my home church at the age of eleven.

How much do you think "Miss Bessie" has been paid over the past seventy-six years? She has never been paid one penny, but she has received great riches knowing that she has served Jesus Christ and the church.

I can never remember one Sunday in my lifetime when the congregation in my home church had to sing without accompaniment because "Miss Bessie" was absent. I can never remember in my lifetime their having to call in a substitute because "Miss Bessie" did not show up. She has always been there. As a matter of fact, she is usually the first one there to open the doors.

There is a beautiful little verse found in Revelation 2:10, "*Be faithful, even to the point of death, and I will give you the crown of life.*" I have a strong feeling that one day the Lord will say to "Miss Bessie," "*Well done, good and faithful servant! You have been faithful with a few things; I will put you in charge of many things. Come and share your master's happiness.*" (Matthew 25:23)

A Cheerful Giver

Her name was Iloise Eliasberg. I met her at the altar of Whitfield Memorial United Methodist Church in Montgomery many years ago. On that particular Sunday morning I had finished preaching a sermon on stewardship with a great emphasis on tithing.

When I gave the invitation, Iloise came forward to join our church. The congregation was singing the closing hymn as she whispered her name in my ear. "I-L-O-I-S-E E-L-I-A-S-B-E-R-G." I could not hear her above the congregational singing, and I presented her as "Mrs. Berg" as we welcomed her into our church family.

When the service ended, Brenda told me that I surely had embarrassed the dear lady and she probably would never return to our church. Brenda insisted that we drive by her residence before we went to lunch so that I could apologize to her.

When we drove by her residence on Price Street and rang her doorbell, she invited us in. I told her how much I regretted introducing her by the wrong name.

She smiled and graciously said, "That is all right. I was in your church for the first time this morning when you spoke on stewardship. God has been good to me through the years and I want to express my love toward Him. At my age there are many things that I physically cannot do, but I can give. I would like to buy new choir robes for your choir members. If you have any children or youth who want to go to Blue Lake Camp this coming summer, I would like to pay their way."

I was moved to tears. The person whom I thought might never return to our church again had overwhelmed me with her spirit of generosity. She took seriously the words the Apostle Paul wrote to the Romans, *"If God has given you money, be generous in helping others with it."* (Romans 12:8 *The Living Bible*)

Down through the years, I have often thought of that unforgettable incident. Stewardship involves all of life and it does include our material gifts. All of us have different degrees of time, talent and financial resources that we can offer to God.

Iloise Eliasberg taught me a valuable lesson long ago. Sometimes when I am too timid to talk about money, I am reminded that there are those persons seated in our pews each Sunday whose hearts overflow with gratitude and simply want an opportunity to give.

Thanks, Iloise, for teaching me a lesson that I shall never forget!

Chapter Three

Memories of Music

Truly Blessed!

Several years ago, while I was visiting in New York City, I attended a Broadway musical that had an intriguing title, *Truly Blessed!* It was a musical based on the life of Mahalia Jackson, the famous black gospel singer from New Orleans who sang in churches from Montgomery, Alabama, to concert halls in New York City. One of the reasons that I enjoyed the musical so much was simply because it contained some of my favorite gospel songs — "Precious Lord, Take My Hand," "Wade in the Water," "He's Got the Whole World in His Hands."

According to the writer of the musical the title came from the meaning of Mahalia, which is *truly blessed!* The famous gospel singer was truly blessed by God with a marvelous voice that inspired Christians all over the world. The Book of Psalms tells us that the Psalmist felt *truly blessed.* He was so overwhelmed as one who felt *truly blessed* that he exclaimed, *"Praise the Lord, O my soul; all my inmost being, praise his holy name."* (Psalm 103:1) *"Give thanks to the Lord, for he is good. His love endures forever."* (Psalm 136:1)

When I complimented an elderly man not long ago on his supportive family, I said to him, "You are surely lucky!" He responded, "No, I am truly blessed."

What about you? Do *you* feel truly blessed?

Leaning on the Everlasting Arms

William Saroyan wrote a novel in 1943 entitled *The Human Comedy*. He told the story of a group of young men on a troop train speeding to the Port of Embarcation for war. As the train rolls along, one of the young soldiers suggests that they sing a hymn. "Which one? "another asks. The young soldier hesitates and then responds "How about that one that goes something like. . . Leaning. . .Yes, you know, 'Leaning on the Everlasting Arms? "'That group of young men began to sing that day aboard the troop train and found new strength that would dispel their greatest fears of what lay ahead.

Ernest Emurian claims that the great gospel hymn with universal appeal, "Leaning on the Everlasting Arms" was first sung in the Pine Log Methodist Church in Bartow County, Georgia. The Reverend Anthony Showalter had been preaching in Hartselle, Alabama, when he received letters from two men who shared with him that they had both lost their wives in death. As this evangelist sat down to write each man a consoling letter, he thought about those words found in Deuteronomy 33:27, "*The Eternal God is your refuge, and underneath are the everlasting arms.*"

Before he finished writing his letters, there flashed into his mind the idea of a gospel song based on that great promise of God. The Reverend Showalter contacted his friend, the

Reverend Elisha A. Hoffman, and requested that he prepare a tune that would fit in with the music and mood of the words he had written. One night in 1888, this new song was sung for the first time in public at the Pine Log Methodist Church.

As we make our pilgrimages through life, I can think of no greater message for us to carry with us than the chorus of this old gospel song,

> Leaning, leaning, safe and secure from all alarms;
> Leaning, leaning, leaning on the everlasting arms.

Singing About Heaven

One of the things that I remember so fondly about my childhood was the celebration of Easter! All of us children in our small community looked forward to Easter afternoon when we would gather at the Wallace Edmonds house across the highway from our home place, and there we would participate in a giant Easter egg hunt! However, on Easter Sunday morning, we would gather in the Emelle Community Church, and there my Uncle Fred, our Sunday School Superintendent, would lead us in the singing of hymns about heaven. I vividly recall how he would be so moved by the Spirit in singing about heaven that he would close his eyes as we sang those familiar favorites from the *Cokesbury Worship Hymnal* — "When They Ring Those Golden Bells," "Shall We Gather at the River," "Sweet By and By," "When We All Get to Heaven," "We're Marching to Zion," "Gathering Home," "The Unclouded Day," and "Beulah Land." "Beulah Land" was probably our favorite of all, simply because following the words of the chorus, "I'm living on a mountain, underneath the cloudless sky," all of the men and children had an opportunity to join in a very strong "*Praise God!*"

Those hymns about heaven made such an impact upon my childhood that I can still recall the page numbers of so many of the Cokesbury hymns. Number 95 was "Beulah Land," number 109 was "When They Ring Those Golden Bells," and number 202 was "Shall We Gather at the River."

73

Philip Yancey, a contemporary Christian writer, claims that in these changing times, people no longer sing, think, or speak about heaven like we once did. He feels that with all of our affluence as a nation, we are prone to say, "Who could ask for anything more?" He reminds us that our secular society no longer sees death as a transition into eternal life and the Biblical images of heaven have lost their appeal to the younger generation. According to his research, streets of gold and gates of pearl spoke to past generations, but those images no longer speak to today's youth.

If Philip Yancey is speaking the truth when he says that people no longer sing, think, or speak about heaven, I am convinced that we are the poorer for it! All of us should be open to learning and singing new hymns, but personally, I still prefer the hymns that speak simply and graphically of that wonderful place called heaven which God has prepared for those who love Him. We long for some imagery of heaven as a beautiful place where one day we might be reunited with our loved ones and friends. That is why Christians for over one hundred years have sung enthusiastically:

> Sing the wondrous love of Jesus,
> Sing His mercy and His grace,
> In the mansions bright and blessed,
> He'll prepare for us a place.

74

Life is Like
a Mountain Railroad

I remember when I was a little boy hearing Roy Acuff sing an old gospel song that included the lyrics:

> Life is like a mountain railroad,
> With an engineer that's brave;
> We must make the run successful,
> From the cradle to the grave;
> Watch the curves, the fills, the tunnels,
> Never falter, never quail;
> Keep your hand upon the throttle,
> and your eye upon the rail.

The words to the chorus are:

> Blessed Savior, Thou wilt guide us,
> Till we reach that blissful shore,
> Where the angels wait to join us,
> In thy praise forevermore.

The words to "Life is Like a Mountain Railroad" were written by W. E. Abbey of Atlanta, Georgia. He was fascinated by trains and saw everything through the eyes of a railroader. He drew a parallel between railroading as he had experienced it in everyday life. He spoke of heaven as the "Union Depot," where the great superintendent waited to welcome the weary pilgrims home.

The music to "Life is Like a Mountain Railroad" was written by a Methodist minister, Charles D. Tillmann, who was born in Tallassee, Alabama, on March 20, 1861. He was converted in a revival in Cuba, Alabama, and became one of the best-known song leaders and evangelists of his day. When he died in Atlanta, the Reverend Tillmann was one of the city's best-loved citizens.

Do you remember that old gospel song? If you do remember it, you may recall the words of admonition near the end,

> Always mindful of obstruction,
> Do your duty, never fail;
> Keep your hand upon the throttle,
> and your eye upon the rail.

Precious Lord, Take My Hand

Thomas A. Dorsey, who wrote the famous gospel song "Precious Lord, Take My Hand," died several years ago in Chicago at the age of ninety-three. Dorsey was born in Villa Rica, Georgia, a small town just off I-20 between Birmingham and Atlanta. His father was a pastor. In 1926, Dorsey composed his first hit, "If You See My Saviour, Tell Him That You Saw Me." He later wrote a song that became a favorite among country music singers, "Peace in the Valley."

In 1931, Dorsey wrote "Precious Lord, Take My Hand" just after his wife died in childbirth and their baby died a day later. Down through the years that great gospel song has served as a constant reminder that we live our lives under the watchful care of a loving Heavenly Father who "neither slumbers nor sleeps."

In the magnificent 139th Psalm, we find these unforgettable words:

Where can I go from your Spirit?
Where can I flee from your presence?
If I go up to the heavens, you are there;
If I make my bed in the depths, you are there.

77

If I rise on the wings of the dawn,
if I settle on the far side of the sea,
even there your hand will guide me,
your right hand will hold me fast.
(Psalm 139:7-10)

The earnest prayer that Thomas Dorsey wrote in a moment of crisis many years ago can strengthen our hearts and lives today.

Precious Lord, take my hand, lead me on, let me stand,
I am tired, I am weak, I am worn;
Through the storm, through the night,
lead me on to the light:
Take my hand, precious Lord, lead me home.

When my way grows drear, precious Lord, linger near,
When my life is almost gone,
Hear my cry, hear my call,
hold my hand lest I fall:
Take my hand, precious Lord, lead me home.

When the darkness appears and the night draws near,
And the day is past and gone,
At the river I stand, guide my feet,
hold my hand:
Take my hand, precious Lord, lead me home.

Nat "King" Cole – A Musical Gift to the World From Our Neighborhood

Nat "*King*" Cole, the world famous musician, was born on March 17, 1919 within walking distance of First United Methodist Church of Montgomery. His father, the Reverend Edward Cole, was serving as pastor of the Beulah Baptist Church and lived at 1524 St. John Street.

When Nat was only a child, he began playing the piano and developed a great love for music. He moved with his parents to Chicago, and it was there that he began his musical career with a jazz band, touring the vaudeville circuit with the "Shuffle Along Revue." In 1937, while in Hollywood, he formed a jazz group, *King Cole Trio,* that spanned three decades and a variety of styles.

Among the songs which made him world famous were "Unforgettable," "Mona Lisa," "When I Fall in Love," "For Sentimental Reasons," "Nature Boy," "It's All in the Game," "Pretend," "Ramblin' Rose," and "Somewhere Along the Way."

One song of Nat "*King*" Cole's that still lives in my memory is "Smile." I recall those lyrics:

Smile, though your heart is aching,
Smile, even though it's breaking,
When there are clouds in the sky,
You'll get by.
If you smile through your fear and sorrow,
Smile and maybe tomorrow,
You'll see the sun
come shining through for you.
You'll find that life is still worthwhile,
If you'll just smile.

Even though the Bible may not teach us specifically about *"smiling,"* the Bible does teach us the root of all smiles, and that is joy found within one's heart. The most wonderful thing about Christian joy is simply that it is not dependent upon outward circumstances of life. Christian joy comes as a gift. The Apostle Paul, from a lonely prison cell in Rome, could write to his Christian friends in Philippi, *"Rejoice in the Lord always. I will say it again: Rejoice!"* (Philippians 4:4)

Nat *"King"* Cole, born in our neighborhood in 1919, spoke for all who put their trust in Jesus Christ:

You'll find that life is still worthwhile
If you'll just smile.

A Solo That Became a Duet

*"Two can accomplish more than twice as much as one,
for the results can be much better. If one falls, the other pulls
him up; but if a man falls when he is alone, he is in trouble."*
(Ecclesiastes 4:9-10 *The Living Bible*)

One of my favorite United Methodist ministers died not
long ago. His name was Don Osgood. A native of Maine, Don
came to Montgomery with the United States Air Force.
Following his tour of duty at Maxwell, Don served for twenty-
five years as a Montgomery police officer, retiring as a major in
1982. Because of his marvelous voice, Don was known among
his peers as "The Singing Policeman." While Don was working
with the Montgomery City Police Department, he felt the call
of God upon his life to enter the United Methodist ministry. In
1982, he became the pastor of the Providence-Harmony Charge
and there he served most effectively for fifteen wonderful years.

Don never had an opportunity to graduate from a
seminary, and he was known in the ministerial world as a local
pastor. Yet he possessed the two greatest qualities for any
minister of the gospel: he loved Jesus Christ, and he loved
people. He passionately wanted the whole world to know of the
redeeming love of God in Jesus Christ.

Don was so proud of his wife, LaMerle, and his two sons, Rocky and Mark. Whenever I complimented Don about either of his sons, he would always say, "That's my boy!" When Rocky graduated from Huntingdon College, he embarked upon a professional singing career, and he now lives in the Boston area where he sings oratorios with some of the most prestigious groups in America. Mark now serves as a fine pastor with our Alabama-West Florida Conference. Several years ago at Annual Conference, when Mark was ordained as a United Methodist minister, the bishop made it clear to the persons being ordained that only an ordained elder could come forward and lay hands upon them. However, when the time came for Mark to be ordained, Don, a local pastor, got up out of the pew, walked up into the chancel area, laid his hands on Mark, and whispered to me on his way back to the pew, "That's my boy!"

My most unforgettable memory of Don took place several years ago at the funeral service for the Reverend B. Gene Williams that was held at the Perry Hill Road United Methodist Church. Our own Lee Jackson had been invited to sing a solo at the funeral. Because of Lee's close relationship with the family of the deceased, he was overcome with emotion in the middle of his solo. It was then that Don did something that will be stamped in my memory forever. Don got up out of his seat, walked up to where Lee was standing, put his arm around him, and all of a sudden, that solo became a duet, as the two of them completed the song together.

82

Perhaps there is someone near you who, for whatever reason, feels that he or she cannot "go on" for another moment. Perhaps it is because that person is dealing with some emotional hurt or pain that has suddenly come upon them. Maybe you will be the one who will get up and put your arm of love around that individual who is hurting so that together your voices can blend into a beautiful song!

This World is Not My Home

Dorothy Thompson wrote an article many years ago concerning what she observed during World War II when American soldiers were in Europe. So many of the young men who served our country were from rural America. The vast majority of them had never been out of their own country, and many of them, before entering the service, had never been out of their home county. A large number of them had attended small rural churches all of their lives before going overseas.

Dorothy Thompson observed that many of the young men were quick to visit Salisbury Cathedral, Notre Dame, or St. Peter's. They stood in awe as they saw the vastness of the domes, the vaulted space filled with light filtering through the stained glass. It awakened in them something of the wonder, grandeur, and mystery of God. They sensed a great Power beyond themselves and were reminded of His loving care.

All of us need to pause periodically and be reminded of the greatness of God. The Bible reminds us that we are pilgrims. Our real home is somewhere else and all of us are marching to a better land.

There is an old gospel song written by Albert E. Brumley entitled "This World Is Not My Home." It contains the lyrics:

This world is not my home,
I'm just a-passing through,
My treasures are laid up
somewhere beyond the blue;
The angels beckon me
from Heaven's open door,
And I can't feel at home
in this world anymore.

O Lord, you know
I have no friend like you.
If Heaven's not my home
then, Lord, what will I do?
The angels beckon me
from Heaven's open door,
And I can't feel at home
in this world anymore*!*

Fill My Cup, Lord!

Richard Blanchard served as a United Methodist minister in the Florida Conference. Several years ago, he wrote a gospel song entitled "Fill My Cup, Lord" that became a favorite of millions of Christians all over the world. One day I was talking with Richard about his composition, and I asked him, "Would you tell me something about the inspiration that you received for writing this song?"

Richard said, "I was serving as a pastor of a church in Coral Gables, and one day I had an appointment with a young couple planning to be married. They were delayed in getting to my office, and so I told my secretary that I was going to walk down the hallway to a Sunday School classroom until they arrived. I sat down at an old upright piano in that Sunday School class, and I started playing. I was there less than thirty minutes when I received the inspiration to write the words and music to that song."

He added, "I was not in a very good mood that day. Everywhere I go, I tell people, 'I was in no mood to be used of God that day, but God was in a mood to use me!' "

Richard told me that the greatest compliment that he ever received from his song came from Queen Elizabeth II of England. During a special religious service for the queen, the queen requested the soloist to sing what she described as her favorite song.

> Like the woman at the well, I was seeking
> For things that did not satisfy.
> And then I heard my Savior speaking,
> "Draw from the well that never will run dry."
>
> Fill my cup, Lord. I lift it up, Lord.
> Come and quench this thirsting of my soul.
> Bread of heaven, feed me 'till I want no more.
> Fill my cup, fill it up and make me whole.

Brighten the Corner Where You Are!

There is an old gospel song entitled "Brighten the Corner Where You Are" that I often heard when I was a child. It was written by Ina D. Ogden in 1913 when she willingly changed her career plans to stay at home with her seriously ill father during the last years of his life. Perhaps some of you remember the lyrics to her song:

> Do not wait until some deed of greatness you may do,
> Do not wait to shed your light afar,
> To the many duties ever near you now be true,
> Brighten the corner where you are.
>
> Brighten the corner where you are!
> Brighten the corner where you are!
> Someone far from harbor you may guide across the bar;
> Brighten the corner where you are!

I have been thinking of the words to that old gospel song in recent days while driving to church each morning and gazing upon the beautiful flowers that Ann Waldo has planted at the "corner" of Carter Hill and Hazel Hedge. Oftentimes I see Ann working among the flowers, and sometimes, if I am lucky, I see her husband Mark, a retired minister, supervising her efforts. I really don't know what has motivated Ann to go the "second mile" to "brighten the corner" where she lives, but one thing I do know, she brightens each day for me when I pass along that way.

There is an old Chinese proverb which reads "It is better to do a good deed at home than to go a thousand miles away from home to burn incense!" The longer I continue in the ministry the more I realize that none of us will ever be able to change the world, but each of us can change our own little part of the world for the better in the places where we live and work each day. If enough of us would seek to *"brighten the corners"* of our own little worlds with seeds of love, encouragement, or understanding, perhaps we might be surprised at the ripple effect those planted seeds might have on others.

Thanks, Ann, for *"brightening the corner where you are!"*

Chapter Four

Memories of Courage

A Little Child Shall Lead Them

Who would have ever dreamed of the tremendous influence that a child with special needs has made upon the lives of thousands of people?

John Paul Miller, son of Dr. and Mrs. J. Carlisle Miller, was born April 2, 1947, in Clanton, Alabama. A handsome child with a very winsome personality, Johnny won a place in the hearts of people in Clanton, Panama City, Montgomery, Dothan, and Mobile where his father served as a United Methodist minister. It is also highly significant that as a result of Johnny's life there now stands in Panama City, Florida, the beautiful Margaret K. Lewis School for Children and Youth with Developmental Disabilities.

When Carlisle was serving as the Montgomery District Superintendent in the early 1960s, he and Irene brought together three other couples to discuss what might be done in Montgomery for special children whose needs were not being met by existing church programs. It was out of that experience that the McInnis School was born. The first classes for the school were held at our First United Methodist Church of Montgomery. A few years later, the McInnis family donated land south of Montgomery where the wonderful McInnis School was built.

In the late 1960s there was a strong desire among the United Methodists of the southeast to do something for people with special needs. Carlisle served as the catalyst in organizing the Southeastern Methodist Agency for Rehabilitation, serving as its first chairman. Literally hundreds of thousands of persons have been touched significantly by this splendid organization. Dr. Robert Pitzer, Executive Director of SEMAR, always gave credit to Carlisle, Irene, and more especially, Johnny, for this great ministry.

Carlisle told me on several occasions, "More good has come through Johnny's life than Irene and I have done in a lifetime." That is a significant statement from two persons like Carlisle and Irene who have touched so many lives.

If you visit the McInnis School in south Montgomery today, you will find a large picture of Johnny hanging in the reception office of the executive director. Johnny died on March 10, 1962.

Dale Evans, the mother of a developmentally-challenged child, wrote a book years ago entitled *Angel Unaware,* and those are the words that Carlisle and Irene chose to place upon the marker where Johnny lies buried in Greenwood Cemetery: "Angel Unaware."

Johnny's life on earth was only fifteen years, but his influence will be felt forever!

Virginia Allison Chappell

There is so much sadness in my heart today because I know how much Henry, Diane and Jennifer must be hurting over the loss of Allison. She was such a remarkable young lady whose whole life centered around Jesus Christ. I was not surprised that in her brief lifetime she had touched so many lives that our large sanctuary could not hold all the people who came to her funeral.

Allison had served as a leader in every area of our church's life—Administrative Board, Council on Youth Ministries, Youth delegate to Annual Conference, Youth Choir, Handbell Choir, and Committee on Nominations and Personnel.

It is little wonder that Allison's peers at Auburn University during her senior year had selected her to be President of Mortar Board and Vice President of War Eagle Girls and Plainsmen. She was named to "Who's Who in American Colleges and Universities." She was also named the "model sister" for her Kappa Delta sorority. A National Merit Finalist with superior academic credentials, Allison was preparing to enter law school in the fall.

Allison carried her Bible with her wherever she went. When she died, her family shared with me a prayer she had written and placed within her Bible. I was deeply moved when

93

I read in her own handwriting this personal prayer that reflects the spiritual maturity of someone far beyond her twenty-two years.

Father God,

I praise you for being a mighty God, all-powerful, all-knowing, all-loving and holy. Thank you for sending your Son to die for me and to cover my sins so that I can have fellowship with you eternally.

I give you all areas of my life — family, school, and career. Give me understanding and strength not to grab them back. Help me keep my eyes on you.

Lord, thank you for the example of the Psalmist David and the quiet strength and beauty of his intimacy with you. Help that to be my ultimate goal.

I ask for wisdom, insight, faithfulness, and strength. I ask for a dependent spirit and a quiet and sure confidence and joy that you will accomplish all things for me in your good time. I count all things as a loss in light of the surpassing value of a life filled with Jesus Christ. Nothing else matters.

I give myself to you.

Your loving and obedient child,
Allison

Thinking About
Leita Coleman

I have been thinking about Leita Coleman so much in recent days. What a marvelous inspiration Leita has been to me through the years! Many of you will recall that one beautiful spring morning in May, 1996, Leita and her husband, Elliott, were riding down to her hometown of Eufaula when they were involved in a terrible head-on collision. Elliott was killed instantly, and Leita was critically injured and rushed to the emergency room at Jackson Hospital.

When I arrived at the emergency room to see Leita, she knew that Elliott had been killed. She was also very much aware that she had multiple broken bones and serious internal injuries. She realized that if she lived, she would be facing months and months of major surgeries and even years of rehabilitation. Leita was transferred to University of Alabama Hospital in Birmingham for the treatment of her critical injuries. Needless to say, the days ahead for Leita appeared very dark and dreary.

However, when I sat down beside Leita's bed in the intensive care unit at UAB and planned the funeral service for her husband, she asked if I might include within the service a quotation that she and Elliott kept on the door of their refrigerator at home.

> The longer I live, the more I realize the impact of attitude on life. Attitude, to me, is more important than facts; it is more important than the past, than education, than money, than circumstances, than failures, than successes, than what other people say or do. It is more important than appearance, giftedness, or skill. It will make or bust a company, a church, or a home. The remarkable thing is that we have a choice each day regarding the attitude that we will embrace for that one day. We cannot change the inevitable; the only thing we can do is play on the string we have, and that is our attitude. I am convinced that life is 10% what happens to me and 90% how I react to it, and so it is with you. You are in charge of your attitude!

Leita underwent approximately twenty major surgeries over the next several years and spent many, many months in rehabilitation. However, she chose to react with a positive attitude that made all the difference in the world. She emerged victoriously from all of her major surgeries and extensive rehabilitations with a radiant spirit that accompanied her warm and contagious smile. Thanks, Leita, for reminding us that even amid the most difficult times of our lives, each of us is in charge of our attitude!

A Miracle of Modern Medicine

A very unusual thing happened one Sunday morning during our 11:00 a.m. worship service. One of our most faithful members, Joanna Byrd, was seated among our worshippers when a telephone call came to our church that a donor had been found for her to have a heart and lung transplant at the University of Alabama in Birmingham. One of our ushers walked down the aisle to where Joanna was seated in the pew and escorted her outside to relay the news. Joanna's husband, David, drove her immediately to Birmingham, and there she underwent eleven hours of surgery that began at 5:30 p.m. on Sunday.

Joanna had been diagnosed with pulmonary hypertension and was in need of a heart and lung transplant. When she was called out of church, she never realized that she would become Alabama's first "domino transplant" recipient. As she received a heart and lungs from a donor, she gave her heart to Vanessa Dickerson of Birmingham, who had suffered a virus that had damaged her heart. Domino transplants can be done only on occasions when the circumstances are right and the heart of the person with the pulmonary disease is not damaged.

The advancements in modern medicine continue to astound the human imagination. As I stand amazed at the very idea of the transplant of a human heart from one life to another, I always stand amazed at the transformation that I have observed when the heart of Christ is transplanted into a human life.

We read in Ezekiel 36:26: *"I will give you a new heart and put a new spirit in you."*

Are you in need of a heart transplant today? If so, why don't you pause long enough to invite Jesus Christ into your heart?

Remembering a
Compassionate Physician

When I was fresh out of seminary, I was appointed to be the associate pastor at the First United Methodist Church of Andalusia, Alabama. Brenda and I loaded up everything we owned in a small "U-Haul," and moved to that delightful Covington county seat town. We arrived in Andalusia late one Saturday evening and spent the night in the old Gables Motel, Andalusia's version of the Ritz-Carlton. All of the people in Andalusia were unusually warm and friendly to us as newcomers, but when you are in a new and strange environment and need a physician, your anxiety level will surely rise. When I called upon Dr. W. Gary Cumbie in my time of need, I discovered a sensitive, compassionate physician that I shall never forget.

Dr. Cumbie delivered babies, set broken limbs, performed surgeries, and treated all kinds of illnesses. He was a surgeon, radiologist, internist, gynecologist, pediatrician, cardiologist, and urologist rolled into one. His doctor's office was located within walking distance of our church. It was not surprising that his waiting room was always filled to overflowing with people from all walks of life, simply because his caring spirit would never let him turn a deaf ear to anyone in need.

99

Dr. Cumbie delivered our first daughter, Stacie, at Andalusia Hospital. As a matter of fact, he and his wife Carolyn spent the whole day with us at the hospital. When Stacie was born, Dr. Cumbie looked at me and said, "Karl, whenever I deliver a baby, I am reminded that God still performs miracles in our world!"

Several years ago, Dr. Cumbie became ill and was hospitalized at Jackson Hospital in Montgomery. A long time friend and admirer of his, Ed Dannelly from Andalusia, came through Montgomery on his way to Auburn the very next day. As he passed through Montgomery, Ed ordered some flowers from Rosemont's to be delivered to Dr. Cumbie's room on Monday morning. When I dropped by to see Dr. Gary Cumbie on Monday, the flowers were there. However, I learned that Ed Dannelly, who had sent the flowers, had died in Auburn the day before the flowers were actually delivered. As I stood there and gazed at those flowers in Dr. Gary Cumbie's hospital room, I thought to myself, "Both the living and the dead give thanks for the good life of this compassionate physician."

As we grow older, and hopefully wiser, we discover, like Henry Nouwen, that individuals who mean the most to us in life are not those who have offered us the greatest advice or solutions to our problems, but rather those individuals who have reached out to us and touched our lives with gentle, caring hands.

John Greenleaf Whittier, in grateful appreciation of a physician in his day, reflected upon the life of Jesus Christ as a Divine Physician. He was inspired to write these lines:

So stood of old the holy Christ,
    amidst the suffering throng,
With whom His lightest touch sufficed,
    to make the weakest strong.

That healing gift He lends to them,
    who use it in His name,
The power that filled His garment's hem,
    is evermore the same.

The good physician liveth yet,
    thy friend and guide to be;
The healer by Gennesaret,
    shall walk the rounds with thee.

Dr. Raleigh H. Pickard —
A True Servant of Jesus Christ
April 8, 1922 — November 25, 1994

God did a beautiful thing on April 8, 1922, when Raleigh Henry Pickard was born in Montgomery, Alabama. His father was a Methodist minister, as was Raleigh's older brother, Bill, and younger brother, Sam. Raleigh graduated from Georgiana High School, received his B. S. degree from Vanderbilt University and his Doctor of Medicine degree at Vanderbilt Medical School. He specialized in ophthalmology, receiving training at Tulane University and his diploma of ophthalmology from Moorefield Eye Hospital in London, England.

On June 12, 1948, Raleigh married Louisa Palmore, daughter of a Methodist minister from Virginia. Raleigh and Louisa were accepted as missionaries by the Board of Missions of the Methodist Church and were assigned to India. They arrived in India with two little girls. Two sons were born in India, and a third son was born in New Orleans while they were there on furlough.

Raleigh served for thirty-two years as a medical missionary in three medical centers in India—Kolar, Yadgiri, and Bidar. The Holston Conference and First United Methodist Church of Montgomery established the hospital and a wing for eye surgery. First United Methodist Church of Montgomery purchased property where the hospital was located.

The property in India was given the name of "Cloverdale" in recognition of the site in Montgomery where our church is located. Housing for the hospital staff was built on the "Cloverdale" property and gardens on the property provided food for the staff and persons in the hospital.

Raleigh established the "Eyes for India" mission program, and thousands of persons recovered their sight physically and spiritually. As a result of his healing ministry among the people of India, there were many whose eyes were opened to Jesus Christ.

While visiting his nephew, the Reverend Jamie Pickard, at Baptist Medical Center in Montgomery, Raleigh suffered a ruptured aortic aneurysm. In the moments following his death, Louisa made sure that Raleigh's eyes were donated, as he had requested, and that his body be given to medical science.

When she called the children to tell them of their father's death, I overhead her say to one of them, "Now I still plan to go from Montgomery to Kentucky and take the items we have for the three Appalachian missions. That is where we were headed when we came through Montgomery."

When we planned the memorial service for Raleigh that was held in our sanctuary, Louisa made only two requests. She said, "I would like for us to sing as an opening hymn the one that Raleigh loved so much, 'To God Be the Glory.' I would also love for you to have someone sing the solo, 'Others.'"

When I reflected upon the seventy-two years that Raleigh Pickard lived upon this earth and his unselfish devotion to Jesus Christ and all humankind, I thought of how appropriate it was that the words to "Others" be sung at his memorial service.

> Lord, help me live from day to day,
> in such a self-forgetful way,
> that even when I kneel to pray,
> my prayer shall be for others,
> Others, Lord, yes, others,
> let this my motto be,
> Help me to live for others,
> that I may live like Thee.

Remembering President Boris Trajkovski of Macedonia

One of the most interesting persons that I ever met was Boris Trajkovski, the President of Macedonia. He was a United Methodist lawyer and lay pastor whom I first met when he was elected a delegate to our General Conference. As President of Macedonia, Boris was presented the World Methodist Peace Award for his role as a peacemaker in Macedonia. In 2001, it appeared for all practical purposes that his country of Macedonia would be torn apart by a conflict with the Albanian rebels. According to the editors of *Time* magazine, it was President Trajkovski who stepped forward for his country and oversaw the peace agreement that held firm when it seemed that peace was impossible in Macedonia.

When Boris Trajkovski was presented the World Methodist Peace Award at a meeting of the Executive Committee of the World Methodist Council in Oslo, Norway, I was privileged to be in attendance. A reception was held in honor of President and Mrs. Trajkovski following the worship service where he received the award. I had an opportunity to meet and talk with President Trajkovski at the reception. He was a handsome man who dearly loved Jesus Christ and the church.

When I returned home to Montgomery and learned a few months later (on February 27, 2004) that President Boris Trajkovski of Macedonia had been killed in a plane crash, I was deeply saddened. Just before he died in the plane crash, though, Boris wrote a devotional and mailed it to *The Upper Room*. It appeared in *The Upper Room* on May 11, 2005. This is what he shared:

> Peace is a noble goal, but, too often, we find that when leaders and politicians talk about striving for peace, they mean merely the absence of war. However, peace as the Bible pictures it is much more than the absence of open conflict.
>
> Psalm 85:10 reads, *'Love and faithfulness meet together; righteousness and peace kiss each other.'* The fruit of genuine faith in Jesus Christ is righteousness and peace, that peace which grows from and builds on righteousness.
>
> If we are truly interested in achieving peace in this world—harmony, tranquility, and freedom from war and its ravages—then we must pursue righteousness. Only when our hearts, minds, motives, and actions are focused on Jesus Christ will we build lasting peace.

A Letter from Mary T. Thompson

One of the great saints of our church, Mary T. Thompson, died on July 28, 2000, at the age of 101. "Miss Mary" embodied that definition of a saint as "one who makes it easier for others to believe in God!" Prior to her death, she wrote a letter to her children and grandchildren that I have found to be a great source of inspiration. I asked permission from her family members to share the contents of her letter with all of you.

My precious children and grandchildren (this includes those who have given their hearts and shared their lives in marriage with them, for I love each one and appreciate the fullness and happiness you have brought to our family).

There is nothing I have wanted more than that you would all live in love, understanding, and helpfulness with each other. There is so much comfort and strength in a close, loving relationship within a family!

There is no material possession which I have to leave any of you that would make a difference in your life, for the greatest possession I have I cannot give you; but it is yours to have if you so desire. That possession is my deep trust, and true appreciation of God's love, providence, and grace. His Spirit has been a guide and a comfort to me in all things — helping me meet and overcome the difficulties, and be more appreciative and thankful for the abundant blessings that have come into my life. There is no strength for life equal to the knowledge of God as revealed through His Son, Jesus Christ, our Lord and Savior. There is no other way for perfect peace in life than to try to follow His way!

How good God has been to give me a long life in which I have been privileged to see my children and grandchildren grow and develop into beautiful maturity! God has put so much love in my heart that it overflows and surrounds each one of you — my precious family — my children, grandchildren, and all the little ones, my great-grandchildren! My love will be with you always, for love never dies!

May God bless and keep each one of you always.

Mother and Grandmama and G.G.

The Sun is Not Set

Henry Ward Beecher once said,

> When the sun goes below the horizon,
> it is not set. The heavens glow for a full hour
> after its departure. And when great people set,
> the sky of the world is luminous long after they
> are out of sight. Such people cannot die out of
> this world. When they go, they leave behind
> them much of themselves.

I thought of those words the other day when I reflected upon the life of Bill Hitchcock. Brenda and I once had the good fortune of being neighbors to Bill and Pat Hitchcock when we lived at the corner of Gladlane and Partridge streets in Montgomery. They were such wonderful neighbors, always going the second mile to check on others within the neighborhood. All of the children adored Bill because each Halloween he would have a big pumpkinfest in his backyard. He would invite all of the children of the neighborhood to be his guests, and he would carve out a pumpkin for each one of them.

Bill's main hobby was working in his yard. He manicured his lawn and planted beautiful shrubbery and flowers all around his home. He was an executive with the local Coca

Cola Bottling Company. Bill was also a "dyed in the wool" Presbyterian who was predestined to live across the street from a United Methodist parsonage.

Bill died on Easter morning. He worked in his yard the last days of his life. When I drove in front of his home the other day, I could not help but smile when I saw the beautiful roses growing in his yard, roses that Bill had planted prior to his death. Once again, I was reminded of the truth of those words of Henry Ward Beecher, "Good people cannot die out of this world. When they go, they leave behind them much of themselves."

In Bill Hitchcock's case, it was beautiful flowers among other things. For someone else it might be a fond memory of a gentle touch, a warm smile, an encouraging word, a kind deed, or a positive influence that manifests itself in a thousand different ways.

There are so many Bill Hitchcocks in all of our lives. Perhaps we need to open our eyes and see the seeds of influence that are blooming all around us. The seeds were planted by those whose voices are now silent, and yet the influence of these persons will be felt forever.

Three Days to See

The singing of the birds outside my window this morning reminds me that spring is on its way! Spring is such a beautiful season of the year, when new life bursts forth all around us, and we open our eyes to the beauty of God's creation.

Helen Keller, one of the greatest Alabamians to ever live on the face of the earth, wrote one of my favorite devotionals, "Three Days to See." She described in detail what she would do during the course of three sighted days, precious moments to a person living in darkness and silence. She shares these thoughts:

I have often thought it would be a blessing if each human being was stricken blind and deaf for a few days at some time during his early adult life. Darkness would make him more appreciative of sight; silence would teach him the joys of sound. I who cannot see find hundreds of things to interest me through mere touch. I feel the delicate symmetry of a leaf. I pass my hands lovingly along the bark of a pine. In spring, I touch the branches of trees hopefully in search of a bud, the first sign of awakening nature after her winter's sleep. I feel the delightful, velvety texture of a flower. Occasionally, if I am very fortunate, I place my hand gently on a small tree and feel the quiver of a bird in full song.

111

I am delighted to have the cool waters of a brook rush through my open fingers. To me a lush carpet of pine needles or spongy grass is more welcome than the most luxurious Persian rug.

I who am blind can give one hint to those who can see: use your eyes as if tomorrow you would be stricken blind. Hear the music of voices, the song of a bird, the mighty strains of an orchestra, as if you would be stricken deaf tomorrow. Touch each object you want to touch as if tomorrow your tactile sense would fail. Smell the perfume of flowers, taste with relish each morsel, as if tomorrow you could never smell and taste again. Make the most of every sense; glory in all the facets of pleasure and beauty.

What would you do if you had only three days to see?

The Trail of Tears

One of the most heartbreaking stories in the history of our nation has to be the story of the "Trail of Tears" that was traveled by 17,000 Cherokee Indians during the cold winter of 1838-39. It was a tragic exodus of a once-proud nation. The Cherokee Indians had lived in the forest-clad mountains and villages of North Carolina, Tennessee, north Georgia, and north Alabama for thousands of years. However, when gold was discovered in north Georgia, the fate of the Cherokee nation was sealed.

While Andrew Jackson was in the White House, the decision was made for the Cherokees to be removed from their lands and begin a six-month trek that would take them 1,200 miles from North Carolina to Oklahoma. As they left North Carolina, they moved through McMinnville, Murfreesboro, and Nashville, Tennessee. They passed near Hopkinsville, Kentucky. They wandered through southern Illinois until they reached the Mississippi River opposite Cape Girardeau. When they were finally able to cross the Mississippi River, they passed through Springfield, Missouri, and a corner of Arkansas before they finally reached northeastern Oklahoma.

More than 4,000 Cherokees died along the "Trail of Tears." It was a trail of hurt, heartache, sickness, and suffering.

The Cherokees traveled approximately ten miles each day, and historians claim that wherever they stopped for the night, they buried fourteen or fifteen of their own. The Cherokees who died along the "Trail of Tears" were buried in unmarked graves in strange and alien soil.

As I reflect upon the "Trail of Tears" that the Cherokees walked many years ago, I am reminded that Jesus Christ, our Lord and Savior, also walked a "Trail of Tears." We read in Luke's gospel, *". . . Jesus resolutely set out for Jerusalem. "*(Luke 9:51) When He neared the Holy City, John's gospel reminds us, *"Jesus wept."* However, there was no turning back as Jesus walked down the Via Dolorosa, the way of sorrows, on His way to the cross.

As we journey toward Jerusalem, let us keep ever before us the sacrificial death of Jesus Christ on the cross for our sins. As we focus upon the "Trail of Tears" that Jesus walked for each of us, let us respond in love and adoration.

This is Livingstone!

David Livingstone inspired the hearts of millions of people all over the world. Shortly after he graduated in 1840 with a medical degree from the University of Glasgow, he left for the dark continent of Africa. There he remained for the next thirty-three years. When he died on April 30, 1873, they brought his body back to London to be given a royal burial. His biographer tells the story of how, on the day of Livingstone's funeral, thousands of people lined the streets of London to pay their respects to this remarkable man. Among them was an old high school classmate of Livingstone's who was overheard to say, "You know, when we were in high school, we thought David Livingstone was a fool." But then he added, "Perhaps we put our emphasis on the wrong things!"

David Livingstone's body was taken to Westminster Abbey for a royal burial. I have always loved the inscription on the marker which designates his final resting place:

He needs no epitaph to guard a name which
men shall prize while worthy work is done.
He lived and died for good. Be that his fame.
Let marble crumble. This is Livingstone.

As we make our pilgrimages through life, we may find it becomes increasingly difficult to establish our priorities and clarify our values. David Livingstone accomplished this task at an early age and recognized the truth of those words of old, "Soon this life will be past; only what is done for Christ will last."

Chapter Five

Memories of Sports

Small Beginnings Can Produce Great Results

I made my very first trip to Green Bay, Wisconsin, the other day. I had heard of Green Bay all of my life, and I was very eager to see for the very first time the city that is home to the Green Bay Packers of the National Football League. When I arrived in Green Bay, I could hardly believe my eyes. Green Bay is only half the size of Montgomery. I was told that you could take all of the citizens of Green Bay and put them inside the Packers' Lambeau Football Stadium.

After I walked through the stadium, I took a tour of the Packers' Hall of Fame. There I discovered a distinct Montgomery flavor with all of the pictures and films of Bart Starr, a Montgomery product who graduated from Sidney Lanier High School. However, the one thing that caught my attention was the stone marker in front of the Packers' Hall of Fame. There was an inscription on the marker which read:

GREEN BAY PACKERS
They acquired their first jerseys by persuading a packing
company to put up money for equipment
and originally, played their games in an open field
where fans 'passed the hat.'
The Green Bay Packers have won 11 world championships,
more than any other club in league history.

118

When I walked away from that marker in that relatively small city in northern Wisconsin, I was reminded once again that, so often, the greatest things in life have the humblest beginnings.

Jesus, in that familiar parable of the mustard seed, reminded us that even within the kingdom of God small beginnings can produce great results. In a world that has adopted the theme "The bigger, the better," God continues to use humble people and places in very significant ways.

When God chose to reveal Himself in human flesh, one would have thought that he would have chosen a city like Rome or Athens for the place of Jesus' birth. Yet, the Bible reminds us that "His ways are not our ways; neither are his thoughts our thoughts." One cattle shed could house all of the people who knew of that first Christmas. Yet, there in the backside of nowhere in the little town of Bethlehem, Jesus Christ was born.

We should always remember that in the eyes of God, there are no insignificant people and places!

I Can Still Smell the Cowhide

Spud Davis is a member of the Alabama Sports Hall of Fame. A native of Birmingham, he was an All-Star catcher in the 1930s and 1940s with the St. Louis Cardinals and Pittsburgh Pirates. He batted over .300 in nine of his sixteen seasons in the major leagues.

Spud Davis would always hunt in the off-season in my hometown. He was an idol for my brothers and me. We would always look forward to following his career during the major league season, but we would especially look forward to the off-season when he would come down from his home in Birmingham to go hunting and tell us how he once caught the fast balls of Dizzy Dean.

One early spring he invited our family to come to Birmingham when his Pittsburgh Pirates broke spring training camp and stopped over to play an exhibition game with the Birmingham Barons at Rickwood Field. There in the old Thomas Jefferson Hotel he introduced us to the then famous Ralph Kiner, a now Hall of Famer who was Spud's teammate with the Pirates.

During the spring of 1946 there arrived at our home a plain-wrapped box that had been mailed from Pittsburgh. You can imagine the excitement I felt when I saw that it was from our hero, Spud Davis. When my brothers and I opened the box, we experienced the thrill of a lifetime. In that box were twelve of the most beautiful gifts I have ever seen in my life — major league baseballs. Each one of the twelve baseballs had grass stains and the imprint of the National League. We were so excited that we could hardly sleep that night. When we were finally in our beds we dreamed of players like Ralph Kiner who may have hit those balls that caused the grass stains. We would take them out of the box several times a day just to smell them and know that they were real.

Spud Davis died in 1984. Each year when the major league baseball season gets into full swing, my mind always goes back to that moment long ago when Spud Davis sent those grass-stained baseballs to my brothers and me.

The Apostle Paul wrote a thank you letter to the Philippians long ago. In that epistle of joy, Paul described the gift that they had sent to him as *". . . a fragrant offering, an acceptable sacrifice, pleasing to God."* (Philippians 4:18)

I do not have any idea what those twelve baseballs cost Spud Davis. Perhaps nothing. However, they were worth more than a million dollars to four little boys. Sometimes even now when I lie down to sleep in the spring and think about that act of loving kindness long, long ago, I can still smell the cowhide!

My Mama Taught Me How to Pray

One of the most remarkable high school athletes that I ever met was Carl Joseph of Madison High School in northwest Florida. He won thirteen athletic letters in football, basketball, baseball, and track. He was six feet tall and weighed one hundred and eighty pounds. He could dunk a basketball, and he could high jump five feet ten inches. He could throw the shot put farther than anyone on the Madison High School track team. The most amazing thing about Carl Joseph is that he had only one leg. He was born that way.

When Carl Joseph was a high school senior, the news of this remarkable high school athlete swept across our nation. He appeared on the "Today Show" of NBC, as well as the television program, "That's Incredible!" He was flown by Bart Starr to Green Bay to be the guest of the Green Bay Packers.

When he graduated from high school, Carl Joseph was offered a scholarship to attend the University of Pittsburgh, even though it was known at the time that he would never be able to play a down. The coaches at the University of Pittsburgh simply wanted him to attend their university to be an inspiration to the football players who were physically able to play football at that level of competition. He later transferred to one of our United

Methodist colleges, Bethune-Cookman in Daytona Beach, and there he became the only one-legged football player in any college in America.

When Carl Joseph graduated from the Madison High School in Madison, Florida, the town declared a Carl Joseph Day. High school and college coaches and professional athletes from all across the nation descended upon that northwest Florida town for the grand celebration. When everybody had finished making their speeches in honor of Carl Joseph he was invited to come to the podium and share a few words. It was then that this humble young man walked to the microphone, and standing on one leg said, "I am not much of a talker, but my Mama taught me how to pray, so let's all pray." The people bowed their heads, and when Carl Joseph finished praying that night, there was not a dry eye in the packed house.

Sometimes we tend to forget that the only request the disciples of Jesus ever made of Him was the simple request, *". . . Lord, teach us to pray. . . ."* (Luke 11:1) Somewhere along the way many years ago, the mother of Carl Joseph made that same simple request, and it was evident that her prayer life had exerted a very positive influence upon the life of her son. Perhaps the heartwarming story of Carl Joseph can remind all of us that we are called not to be "talkers" but to be "listeners" to the still, small voice of God.

"How Tall is a Giant?"

Little League Baseball has swept the imagination of people all over the world. Today there are millions of Little League players in the U. S. and many foreign countries. Each summer these little boys play for local, district, and regional championships, until in August the World Series of Little League Baseball is held in Williamsport, Pennsylvania.

The action in 1957 was particularly dramatic, for in that year there was a group of little boys from Monterrey, Mexico, who won the title "South of the Border" and went away to McAllen, Texas, to play in the regional championship. Before they left home, the Lions Club in Monterrey prepared a banquet in their honor, because everyone knew they would be defeated and return home. However, these little boys won 10 consecutive games as they won the right to play in the World Series of Little League Baseball in Williamsport.

What made the story so dramatic was the unusual small size of the 14 little boys! They averaged only four feet, eleven inches in height and their average weight was ninety-two pounds. The players came from poverty stricken homes and carried paper bags for suitcases. They rode a dilapidated bus all of the way from Monterrey to Williamsport.

They beat Bridgeport, Connecticut, in the semifinal game, 2-1, and then something very dramatic took place. Monterrey had a 12-year-old, 88-pound boy, by the name of Angel Marcias. This ambidextrous kid who had played the semifinal game at first base left-handed pitched the final game right-handed against LaMesa, California. Not only did Monterrey win 4-0, but Angel Marcias pitched a perfect game, winning the World Championship.

The New York Times the next morning had a headline article with the caption, "**Unbelievable!**" The 14 little boys were flown to New York City for TV appearances, to Washington D.C. to meet the President, and to Monterrey where over 100,000 fans welcomed them home. Each boy's family was given a lot on which to build a home, and each of the boys was given a scholarship to the finest private institution in Mexico. Shortly after these little boys won the World Championship, a movie "How Tall is a Giant?" was made of this inspiring story. Near the end of the movie, the answer to that question was given, "A giant is as tall as three things — faith, courage, and a dream." The same can be said of Christian giants — faith in Jesus Christ, courage to overcome all obstacles of life, and a dream of how one might be used in service to others. Harry Kemp once said, "The poor man in life is not he without a cent, but the poor man in life is he without a dream." George Bernard Shaw wrote "Some men see things as they are and say, 'Why?' I dream things that never were and say 'Why not?'"

A Short Season

One of the most amazing college football players who ever performed on the gridiron was a young man by the name of Brian Piccolo. A native of Fort Lauderdale, Florida, Brian Piccolo won a scholarship to Wake Forest University where he became an All-American and led the Atlantic Coast Conference in rushing and scoring. As Piccolo starred on the gridiron on Saturday afternoons, the sportswriters in North Carolina had a field day with the headlines in the sports pages on Sunday morning — "Piccolo Plays To Winning Tune!"... "Little Piccolo Plays Like 76 Trombones!"..."The Sweetest Music This Side of Heaven Comes From A Piccolo!"

After a sensational career at Wake Forest, Brian Piccolo signed with the Chicago Bears and found himself a substitute for Gale Sayers. However, Piccolo finally got his chance to play one day when Gale Sayers was injured and the Chicago Bears were preparing to play the Atlanta Falcons. In that game with the Atlanta Falcons, Brian Piccolo developed a cough and pains that were later diagnosed as cancer. When he returned to Atlanta for his last visit, Piccolo invited the minister who had officiated at his wedding to come to his hotel room and serve communion to him, his wife Joy and their three young daughters.

Brian Piccolo died on June 16, 1970, but his life has been an inspiration to people all over this nation. Several years ago, a book entitled *Brian Piccolo: A Short Season* was written about his life. It was made into a movie entitled *Brian's Song*. The simple message of the book and movie was that the twenty-six years of Brian Piccolo's life were such "a short season" for someone who had so much to offer to this world.

The Bible reminds us that all of us have "short seasons." The writer of James asked, *"What is your life? You are a mist that appears for a little while and then vanishes."* (James 4:14) The Psalmist compares each of our lives to grass that flourishes in the morning, but under the heat of the sun, it withers and fades in the evening. In that magnificent 90th Psalm we read *"For a thousand years in your sight are like a day that has just gone by, or like a watch in the night. . . . Teach us to number our days aright, that we may gain a heart of wisdom."* (Psalm 90:4,12) Thomas Carlyle spoke of our lives as a "gleam of light between two great eternities." When we pause long enough to realize that all of us, even if we live to be 100, have short seasons upon this earth, we can affirm these words of the Psalmist, *"This is the day the Lord has made; let us rejoice and be glad in it!"* (Psalm 118:24)

Stamina and Perseverance

One of the greatest needs within the life of the church today is the need for stamina and perseverance. Norman Vincent Peale reminded us in *The Power of Positive Thinking* that our whole lives could be changed if we would repeat ten times aloud each day those words of the Apostle Paul, *"I can do everything through him who gives me strength."* (Philippians 4:13)

I love the story of the undefeated football team at the University of the South (Sewanee, Tennessee) in 1889. They had a 12-0 record that year with an all-male student body of ninety-seven students. They beat Georgia Tech 32-0, the University of Tennessee 46-0, and Southwestern 54-0.

However, the most amazing thing about their undefeated season was their famous road trip covering three thousand miles in which they won five games in six days. On November 8, they beat the University of Texas in Austin 12-0. On November 9, they beat Texas A&M in College Station 10-0. On November 10, they defeated Tulane in New Orleans 23-0. On November 11, a Sunday, they paused to worship. On November 12, they defeated LSU in New Orleans 40-0. They concluded their road trip on November 13, beating Ole Miss in Oxford 12-0.

They had only twelve players that made the trip. There were eleven who played both ways (offense and defense) with only one substitute. They scored 97 points and held all of their opponents scoreless.

When I think of the perseverance exemplified in the lives of twelve players who led the University of the South to an undefeated season in 1889, I always think of the Apostle Paul. He had every reason to become discouraged and give up in despair, yet he used the metaphor of an athlete when he penned those lines, *". . . Forgetting what is behind and straining toward what is ahead, I press on toward the goal to win the prize for which God has called me heavenward in Christ Jesus."* (Philippians 3:13-14)

Let us with perseverance run the race of life that is set before us!

It is Not What You Accomplish in Life, but What You Overcome That Makes the Difference!

One of the most admired personalities in the world of sports today is a professional golfer whose name is Paul Azinger. When he graduated from Florida State University, "Zinger" became a rising star on the professional golf tour. However, in the midst of his movement toward the top of the golfing world, "Zinger" discovered that he had cancer. He was forced to leave the tour for several months as he valiantly fought the dreadful disease. Through the efforts of compassionate physicians and prayerful friends, Paul Azinger made a comeback. He described what has happened in his life with some insightful words, "A letter from Johnnie Miller came as a turning point in my life. Johnny Miller wrote me, 'It is not what you accomplish in life, but what you overcome that makes the difference.'"

A disease does not discriminate. It is not a respecter of persons. However, all of us can overcome our trials and tribulations of life if we put our faith and trust in Jesus Christ, who triumphed over the worst that life had to offer.

Olive Ann Burns wrote a novel *Cold Sassy Tree* while she was recovering from leukemia. The story is set in north Georgia at the turn of the century. The main character is Grandpa E. Rucker Blakeslee. One of the most unforgettable parts of the book comes at the point where Grandpa E. Rucker Blakeslee gives his definition of the Christian faith. "Faith ain't no magic wand or money back gar'ntee. Hit's jest a way of livin'.... And I found out a long time ago, when I look on some hardship or burden that seems too heavy to carry... I can look on the same thang as a challenge. It is like you done entered a contest. Hit even gits excitin', waitin' to see how everythan's go'n turn out."

I would encourage you to remember today that it is not what you accomplish in life, but what you overcome that makes the difference!

The Home of The 12ᵗʰ Man

Texas A&M University in College Station, Texas, is a university that is rich in tradition. After having made my first visit to Texas A&M, I know now why they say, "Once an Aggie, always an Aggie."

Texas A&M is called "The Friendliest Campus Anywhere." The students greet each other and visitors with a genuine "Howdy." Their mascot is a full-bred American collie named Reveille. The first Reveille died in 1944 and was buried at the west end of Kyle Field in such a place where he can supposedly see and always read the scoreboard from his grave through the portal of the stadium.

One of the great traditions of Texas A&M is their yell leaders, or cheerleaders, at football games. These three seniors and two juniors, chosen by the student body, are always dressed in white. Whenever Texas A&M scores a touchdown, an Aggie is supposed to kiss his date.

However, the greatest tradition at Texas A&M is expressed in a large inscription that reaches from one end of the stadium to the other, "The Home of The 12ᵗʰ Man." Where did this tradition begin?

In 1922, Texas A&M was playing Centre College in the Dixie Classic in Dallas, Texas. E. King Gill, a student at Texas A&M, was sitting in the stands near the end of the first half when he was called to report to the Texas A&M bench. There had been a number of injuries to the Aggies, and Coach Dana X. Bible summoned E. King Gill to put on a uniform and be ready to go into the game.

E. King Gill and one of the injured players went back under the stands. There were no dressing rooms in those days, and visiting teams always dressed in the hotel before the game. There under the stands E. King Gill put on the injured player's uniform and prepared to go into the game, and the injured player put on the clothes of E. King Gill. Today the entire student body stands throughout the game as a tribute to the spirit and loyalty exemplified in the life of E. King Gill many years ago when he was standing in the wings to do his part.

There is a beautiful story in the Bible of a man named Barnabas who was also "standing in the wings" to offer encouragement. His very name means "Son of Encouragement" and wherever his name is mentioned in the Book of Acts, he is offering encouragement. It was Barnabas who sold a field and laid the proceeds at the apostles' feet to be distributed to those in need. It was Barnabas who stepped forward to speak a word of affirmation on behalf of Paul after his conversion. It was Barnabas who was willing to give John Mark a second chance.

133

Yes, it is said of Barnabas that in the worst of times, he did the best of things.

If there is one thing that our world needs today, it is more persons standing in the wings doing their part to offer a word of encouragement. Our world is filled with critics and complainers. However, there is always someone near you who needs a word of encouragement. In light of this, is there someone around you today for whom you can play the role of The 12th Man?

Unsung Heroes

One of the most dramatic football games that I can ever remember was the University of Alabama's 16-15 victory over Georgia Tech at Grant Field in Atlanta on November 12, 1960. Georgia Tech totally dominated the first three quarters, and with only six minutes remaining in the game, Alabama trailed by a score of 15-0. When Alabama's starting quarterback Pat Trammell suffered an ankle injury during that final quarter he was forced to leave the game.

It was then that my good friend Bobby Skelton from Pell City came into the game as quarterback and led Alabama to two long touchdown drives in the final six minutes, closing the gap to 15-13. When Alabama kicked off to Georgia Tech, the Crimson Tide held the Yellow Jackets on downs and took over at Georgia Tech's 45-yard line with less than a minute to play. Bobby Skelton hit Butch Wilson with a 33-yard pass, placing the ball at the 12-yard line.

As the final seconds began to tick away and Alabama had no time-outs left, their only hope was to kick a field goal. Tommy Brooker, the regular field goal kicker, was nursing an injured leg and standing on the sideline on crutches. In the frenzy of the moment, Coach Bryant turned around and yelled for Richard "Digger" O'Dell to go into the game and attempt the field goal.

Richard O'Dell had never kicked a field goal in his life. As the final seconds ticked away Richard O'Dell, who was reared in Lincoln, only eight miles down the road from where Bobby Skelton was reared in Pell City, whispered to Bobby, his holder for the field goal attempt, "Lean her back a tad, and I will kick her through." As the final gun sounded, Richard O'Dell's knuckleball with a trajectory barely high enough to get across the crossbar, sailed through the goal posts. Alabama had scored an incredible 16-15 victory.

During all of the confusion that occurred in the final seconds Maury Ferrell, the Alabama announcer, mistakenly gave credit to the injured Tommy Brooker for the winning field goal. Even when the University of Alabama team arrived back at the airport in Birmingham, hundreds of screaming fans made their way through the crowd to hug Tommy Brooker. The unsung hero, Richard O'Dell, quietly made his way to the bus for the ride back to Tuscaloosa. It was the only field goal that O'Dell would ever attempt in a college football game.

As I reflect upon that unforgettable event, I am reminded that we live in a world of so many unsung heroes like Richard O'Dell. I see these unsung heroes daily, volunteering their time and talents in all walks of life. Isn't it amazing what can be accomplished in a church, a civic club, or any organization when persons care less who gets the credit? Perhaps all of us need to pause periodically and give thanks to God for the unsung heroes in our lives!

Jim Fyffe...
The Voice of the Auburn Tigers!

College football players are reporting for fall practice this week, and I have been thinking about Jim Fyffe, the "Voice of the Auburn Tigers," who was recently inducted into the Alabama Sports Hall of Fame. I had the privilege of joining Rose Fyffe and the family, along with many of Jim's close friends, in Birmingham for that grand occasion.

Jim was born and reared in the very small community of Keaton in eastern Kentucky, just down the road from Redbush and Mazie. As a small boy, Jim had a great dream of becoming a sports broadcaster at a major university. He attended Flat Gap High School that did not even have a high school football team. However, as a teenager Jim began broadcasting high school basketball games around Paintsville where his brother owned the radio station. After receiving a degree in broadcasting from the University of Kentucky, Jim served a tour of duty in the United States Army. When he was discharged from the Army, Jim embarked upon a broadcasting career with WYDE Radio in Birmingham. In 1973, Jim moved to Montgomery to become the sports director of WCOV-TV.

During those early years in Montgomery, Jim called "peewee" football games that were telecast on Saturday mornings from a vacant lot off Adrian Lane near the television station. He also broadcast high school football games, Huntingdon College basketball games, Montgomery Rebel baseball games, and even "professional rasslin!" It was in 1981 that Jim got the biggest break of his life and was named the "Voice of the Auburn Tigers." Jim later wrote in his autobiography, "From the little community where I grew up in Keaton, Kentucky, to Jordan-Hare Stadium is six hundred miles, but in broadcast terms, it is light years."

One of the things that made Jim so very special was his sense of humility. There was no pretense in his life. He never forgot his humble roots. When Jim's career with the broadcasting industry began to skyrocket and his voice was recognized by many sports fans across our nation, Jim did not change. Even when Auburn played Saturday night football games in places like Baton Rouge and Fayetteville and returned home after midnight, Jim was seated in our sanctuary on Sunday morning. He always had a genuine desire to reach out to others. Scott Scoggins, a Selma teenager who was suffering from spinal bifida, shared with Jim that he wanted to become a broadcaster. Jim invited Scott to come and sit beside him in the press box at Jordan-Hare Stadium as he broadcast football games. Jim genuinely felt that he had been richly blessed in life, and he truly wanted to be a blessing to others.

Jim had such a great sense of humor. I loved the story that he told about Bill France of NASCAR fame. Jim was the public address announcer at the Talladega Speedway for a major race. An invocation was listed on the agenda, but the minister who was supposed to give the invocation did not show up. Bill France leaned over and whispered to Jim that he would give the invocation himself. According to Jim, it was obvious that Bill France did not attend church on a regular basis. Bill France started thanking God for the sun and the moon, the birds and the bees, the trees and the flowers, and just when he got into the middle of his prayer, it was obvious that Bill France did not know how to close it. Jim claimed that he could hardly believe his ears when he heard Bill France come to the close of his prayer and simply say, "Sincerely yours, Bill France."

The voice of Jim Fyffe was silenced after fifty-seven years, and yet we know that whenever Auburn fans gather to cheer on their favorite Tigers, they will always remember his signature call, "Touchdown Auburn!" Jim always closed his broadcast of each game with the same unforgettable words, "My time is up! I thank you for yours!"

Those simple words seem so appropriate for a humble servant who graduated from a high school that did not even have a football team, and yet, following a great dream and lots of hard work, became "The Voice of the Auburn Tigers!"

Remembering
Jimmy Hitchcock

Jimmy Hitchcock was born on June 26, 1911, in the small rural community of Inverness, approximately ten miles south of Union Springs, not too far from Blue's Old Stand and Smut Eye. His father operated a general mercantile store. When Jimmy was only five years old, his family moved to Midway where he attended elementary school. Jimmy graduated from high school in Union Springs before heading to Alabama Polytechnic Institute (Auburn University). He became the first All-American at Auburn in 1932. As a great running back, he never weighed more than 160 pounds.

Shortly after graduation from Auburn, Jimmy signed a professional baseball contract with the New York Yankee organization. It was during spring training of 1936 in Florida that Jimmy met and fell in love with Dot Shawkey, the daughter of Bob Shawkey. Bob Shawkey was a pitcher for the Yankees and later became the manager of the Yankees. Following his athletic career, Jimmy and Dot became very active members of our First United Methodist Church of Montgomery.

Whenever I visited with Dot Hitchcock and Jimmy, III, in their home, I always saw the trophies, plaques, and pictures, and even a 1927 World Series ring of the New York Yankees.

140

As I read the numerous newspaper clippings about this active Christian layman, born and reared in rural Bullock county, I thought of how the God of the Bible chose unknown persons in unknown places to carry out His divine purposes. It is very evident that Jimmy Hitchcock never felt that he was at a disadvantage growing up in rural Bullock County. He was determined to be the best athlete he could possibly be. When I walked out the front door of the Hitchcock home, the words of an old poem kept ringing in my ears:

> If you can't be a pine on the top of the hill,
> be a shrub in the valley,
> but be the best little shrub by the side of the hill.
> Be a bush if you can't be a tree.
> If you can't be a bush, be a bit of the grass,
> and some highway happier make.
> If you can't be a muskie, then just be a bass,
> but the happiest bass in the lake.
>
> We can't all be captains. There's got to be a crew.
> There's something for all of us here.
> There's big work to do, and there's lesser to do.
> And the task we must do is the near.
>
> If you can't be a highway, then just be a trail.
> If you can't be a sun, be a star.
> For it isn't by size that you win or you fail,
> But be the best of whatever you are.

Charley Boswell: The Greatest Blind Golfer in the World!

Charley Boswell is remembered today as one of Alabama's greatest sports heroes. He was born and reared in Ensley where he was a star athlete at Ensley High School.

Charley won a football scholarship to the University of Alabama where he was a tailback for Coach Frank Thomas and the Crimson Tide in 1938 and 1939. He also played baseball and ran track at the University of Alabama. He dreamed of playing professional baseball, but he was drafted into the Army.

On November 22, 1944, in the midst of World War II, Charley Boswell was serving as a twenty-seven-year-old Captain in the Ruhr Valley of Germany. While he was riding in a Sherman tank, the tank was hit by enemy fire. Charley Boswell was able to get out of the rear hatch, but he went back to help rescue an eighteen-year-old comrade when the tank was hit a second time.

Charley Boswell was critically wounded and woke up seven days later in an American General Hospital in Heerlen, Holland. A few days later, he was told by a physician that he would be blind for the rest of his life.

While continuing to recuperate from his wounds at Valley Forge Hospital in Pennsylvania, Charley Boswell became severely depressed. In the midst of his depression, a young corporal, Kenny Gleeson, walked into his hospital room and said, "Let's go play some golf." Charley Boswell became exceedingly angry at the young man's insensitivity. However, when Charley Boswell became physically stronger, he told the young man that he would like to play a round of golf with him.

Charley Boswell became the greatest blind golfer in the world, winning twenty-eight national and international tournaments. He once made a hole-in-one on the fourteenth hole at the Vestavia Country Club in Birmingham.

Charley Boswell raised over $1.5 million for the Eye Foundation Hospital in Birmingham through his charity golf tournaments. Today in Alabama, thousands of persons can see because of surgeries performed on their eyes that were paid for with these funds.

If you ever heard Charley Boswell speak, you probably remember his favorite story. It was the time that he challenged Bob Hope to a round of golf, even offering Bob Hope strokes just as long as Charley Boswell could name the place and time. When Bob Hope agreed, Charley Boswell said, "We will play in Birmingham and tee off at midnight." One thing that I remember about Charley Boswell is that each time I had a chance to meet him, he always said, "It is so nice to see you!"

The story of Charley Boswell reminds us of the story of Easter. Easter enables us to look beyond the darkness of this world and with the eyes of faith catch a glimpse of the light of eternity. Easter also enables us in the midst of our depression to find hope for the living of tomorrow. When tragedies come our way and we want to seal our tombs and bury our hopes, God comes to us in the power and presence of the Risen Christ and turns our darkness into light. That is why we shout "Hallelujah! Christ is Risen!"

Remembering Dusty Rhodes

The 1954 World Series between the New York Giants and the Cleveland Indians featured three stars from Alabama: Willie Mays from Fairfield, Early Wynn from Hartford, and Dusty Rhodes from Mathews. However, it was James Lamar "Dusty" Rhodes, born in nearby Mathews on May 13, 1927, who became a national hero and was named the Most Valuable Player.

Dusty Rhodes had been drafted in the twentieth round by the New York Giants. A left-handed batter, he was an outfielder with the Giants from 1952 until 1957. As a pinch hitter in the 1954 World Series he led the Giants to a sweep of the Indians. He was four for six with two home runs and seven RBIs. His role as a pinch hitter has never been forgotten among old-timers, and his name today is enshrined forever in the hearts of Giant fans.

I had the privilege of visiting with Dusty Rhodes at his retirement home in Henderson, Nevada. He shared with me his fond memories of playing baseball at the old Pike Road High School that propelled him on a professional baseball career that culminated in his being named the Most Valuable Player of the 1954 World Series as a result of his pinch-hitting.

145

My dictionary defines a "pinch hitter," as "one who replaces the scheduled batter, especially when a hit is needed." Just like the game of baseball, there is a great need for pinch hitters in every church. One of the most inspiring things that I have observed as a minister down through the years has been the countless number of persons who are willing to "step up to the plate" and substitute when they are needed the most.

Who are these pinch hitters? They are those young adults who show up in a "pinch" and say to a friend injured in an accident, "Let me help with your children." They are the middle-aged adults who learn of a neighbor who has been called out of town because of the death of a loved one, and they quickly respond saying, "Let me volunteer for you this week!" They are the older adults who learn of a family facing a terrible financial crisis and they respond immediately saying, "Would you give me the privilege of helping in that situation?" What in the world would we do today without all of these effective "pinch hitters?"

Dusty Rhodes inspired the world of sports with his heroics as a "pinch hitter" in the 1954 World Series. All of us are greatly inspired today by "pinch hitters" who "step up to the plate" at just the right time and come through in the clutch for us! Is there someone near you for whom you could "pinch hit" today?

Going, Going, Gone!

My favorite sports announcer for many years was Mel Allen, the voice of the New York Yankees from 1939 until 1964. Our own Dot Hitchcock's father, Bob Shawkey, was manager of the Yankees during those years when Mel Allen first began broadcasting. When I was a little boy, I loved to hear Mel Allen describe a home run with his unique expression, "Going, going, gone!" His second well-known expression was simply, "How about that?"

Mel Allen was born on February 13, 1914, in Birmingham. As a junior in law school at the University of Alabama, he broadcast his first college football game between the University of Alabama and Howard College. By 1937 he was a staff announcer with CBS. He announced twenty World Series, twenty-four All-Star games, fourteen Rose Bowls, five Orange Bowls, and two Sugar Bowls. He was best known to younger fans through his syndicated show, "This Week in Baseball" which began in 1977. He was inducted into the Alabama Sports Hall of Fame in 1974.

When Mel Allen died at the age of 82 at his home in Greenwich, Connecticut, Yogi Berra said, "Mel Allen never knocked a ballplayer. He never second-guessed. He always looked for the good in others. He always had something positive to say about everyone!"

147

When I read those words of Yogi Berra describing Mel Allen, I could not help but think of those words that the Apostle Paul wrote to the Philippians, *". . . whatever is true, whatever is noble, whatever is right, whatever is pure, whatever is lovely, whatever is admirable — if anything is excellent or praiseworthy — think about such things."* (Philippians 4:8)

Perhaps the words of the Apostle Paul and the actions of Mel Allen are things that all of us need to remember. Let us always look for the good in others!

An Olympic Memory

One of the most dramatic moments in the history of sports occurred in the summer of 1936, when the Olympic games were held in Berlin, Germany. A twenty-two year-old native Alabamian by the name of Jesse Owens won four gold medals before a crowd of 120,000 persons that included none other than Adolph Hitler. The story actually began on September 12, 1913, when James Cleveland Owens was born in Oakville, Alabama. When he was a child, his family moved to Cleveland, Ohio. When he entered school there, a teacher asked him his name, and he replied, *"J.C."* The teacher thought he had said "Jesse,"and for the rest of his life, he was known by the name that his elementary school teacher gave him.

Jesse Owens attended Ohio State University. It was on May 25, 1935, that he became a national hero. Competing in the Big Ten Championship, Jesse Owens set three world records, and tied a fourth. It was not surprising that the following year this native Alabamian was chosen to be a part of our nation's Olympic team.

Wearing the red, white, and blue of America, Jesse Owens carried our hopes to display his talents before Adolph Hitler, a man who hoped to conquer the world. Jesse Owens described the emotions that he felt as he stepped to the starting line in the 100-meter finals.

149

"My eyes wandered across the field. I noticed the green grass, the red track with the white lines, and as my eyes wandered into the stands I saw 120,000 people standing within that great arena. I thought of my family and friends thousands of miles away back home, and I prayed to God that He would be with me every step of the way." God was with him every step of the way. Not only did he win the 100-meter finals, but he also won three other gold medals in those 1936 Olympics, only to be snubbed by Adolph Hitler.

In 1970 I attended the Annual Induction Dinner of the Alabama Sports Hall of Fame in Birmingham, and one of the eight inductees that night was Jesse Owens. It was an experience that I shall never forget.

One of the places that I later visited in Berlin was the Olympic Stadium, the site of the 1936 Olympics where Jesse Owens had won his four gold medals. As the tour guide drove us around the stadium, he pointed out to us the name of a nearby street. I could hardly believe my eyes when I saw that it was the "Jesse Owens Street."

The writer of Hebrews used the metaphor of the great Olympic games to describe our race through life. He said, ". . . *let us run with perseverance the race marked out for us. Let us fix our eyes on Jesus, the author and perfecter of our faith...."* (Hebrews 12:1-2)

A Ten-year-old's Dying Request
—"Pass Right!"

One of the most heartwarming stories that I have read from the world of sports was the story of a ten-year-old boy, Montana Mazurkiewicz, who lived in Mishawaka, Indiana. It was discovered that Montana had an inoperable brain tumor and was given only a few months to live. Montana was named after Joe Montana of Notre Dame football fame, and was reared to be a great fan of the Fighting Irish.

When Coach Charlie Wies, Head Football Coach at Notre Dame, heard about this young boy named Montana, who had only a brief time to live, the coach made the decision to visit him at his home. Coach Wies took the little boy a Notre Dame football, a couple of t-shirts, and a hat. He discovered when he arrived at the boy's home that the child was paralyzed from the waist down. His mother was rubbing the little boy's shoulder to ease his pain. The child was so weak that he could not even lift the football that was given to him. Coach Wies climbed into the reclining chair with the little boy and threw the football back and forth to his mother Cathy.

When Coach Wies prepared to leave the little boy's home he reminded young Montana that in three days (September 24, 2005) the Fighting Irish would be playing the

University of Washington in Seattle. Coach Wies asked him the question, "Would you like to call the first play in this Saturday's game against Washington?" The little boy said, "Yes, I want to call 'Pass Right!' "Coach Wies went back to South Bend and told the team about his visit earlier in the day with Montana. He also told the team that the very first play of the game against Washington would be the play that Montana called— *"Pass Right."*

The team flew to Seattle to play against the University of Washington. On Thursday night before the game, Montana died. On Saturday, when the Fighting Irish gained possession of the football for the very first time following a fumble, they found themselves on their own one-yard line. Brady Quinn, the Notre Dame quarterback, with a puzzled look, asked Coach Wies, *"What are we going to do now that we are backed up to our own end zone?"*

Coach Wies said, *"We have no choice! We're throwing it to the right!"* On the first play of the game, Brady Quinn threw a pass to the right to Anthony Facano for thirteen yards.

Following Notre Dame's 36-17 victory over the University of Washington, the whole Notre Dame football team signed the game ball while flying home from Seattle. On the following day, Coach Wies went back to Montana's home in Mishawaka, Indiana, and presented the game ball to Montana's mother. She said of Coach Wies, "He is a very compassionate man. I just thanked him for using that play no matter the circumstances."

What motivated this act of compassion on the part of Coach Wies? For one thing, his daughter Hanna has global development delay, a rare disorder similar to autism. Perhaps individuals like Coach Wies who have children who suffer are always more compassionate towards others. Compassion has been defined as "the deep feeling of sharing the suffering of another and the strong desire to give aid or support."

The Apostle Paul put compassion at the top of his list of qualities among those who claim to be followers of Jesus Christ. Writing to the Colossians, Paul penned these words, *"Therefore, as God's chosen people . . ., clothe yourselves with compassion... ."* (Colossians 3:12)

Brenda's Baseball Cards

One of the big laughs around our house surrounds Brenda's baseball card collection from her childhood. She was an avid collector of Topps' cards that came with bubble gum in the late 1950s. She even made her own wooden box, painted it green, and *"cut up"* cards of several famous players to decorate the outside of her prize collection.

Not long ago, we sat down with Dr. James Beckett's *Official Guide for Baseball Cards* to determine the value of her prize collection, hoping that it might provide much-needed funds for our retirement years. If was then that we made a most interesting discovery concerning the worth of the famous baseball players' cards that she *"cut up"* to decorate her box. Among those cards that felt the slice of her childhood scissors were Sandy Koufax ($135.00), Mickey Mantle ($90.00), Ted Williams ($60.00), and Willie Mays ($36.00). However, she kept in perfect mint condition Walt Dropo ($3.50), Frank House ($3.50), Frank Bolling ($6.00), and Vito Valentinetti ($2.50).

So often in life, we discard those most valuable things of life while holding on to the least valuable, realizing only many years later the true worth of the things that slipped through our fingertips. Perhaps the realization comes many years later when we look back over the picture of a family member, friend, neighbor, or a church.

Why not pause today and offer a prayer of thanksgiving for those people all around you who are treasures in your life? Why not use today as an opportunity to express to them their great worth in your life? The greatest treasures that all of us possess are not found in material possessions, but rather in the faces of people.

You're So Right, Carl!

One of our fine members, Carl Stephens, retired as Operations Manager/Program Director of WSFA-TV. He was a faithful member of the WSFA team for almost forty-two years. In addition to making his regular appearance each weeknight on WSFA during the six o'clock and ten o'clock reports, Carl also served as the public address announcer for all of Auburn's home football games. Carl's face and voice became familiar to hundreds of thousands of people scattered across the State of Alabama.

Carl served as host of the Auburn Football Review for the last thirteen years (1963-75) of Coach Ralph "Shug" Jordan's tenure at Auburn University. It was a live, one-hour telecast sponsored by Southern Bell at five o'clock each Sunday afternoon. A film of every play of the previous day's game was shown while Coach Jordan and Carl made their comments. There were only four commercials, one minute in length, during the whole hour.

College football fans of my generation will always remember one comment that Coach Jordan would make, without fail, on the show each Sunday afternoon for thirteen years. As Carl Stephens, the host, would share some insight pertaining to the game, Coach Jordan would always respond, "You're so right, Carl!"

I have thought of those affirming words of Coach Jordan so much in recent days. Sadly enough, we are living in a day and age in which there is an alarming increase in negative reporting. Airways of television and radio have been infiltrated with faultfinding and constant criticism of individuals. The popularity of talk show hosts today is often dependent upon who can engage in the greatest "put-down." In a society like ours, it is not surprising that one of the best-known writers in America, Scott Peck, has chosen to write a book about the loss of civility in our culture.

Living in these changing times, I would like to suggest to you that the Bible has a lot to say about our need to affirm one another. The whole letter of Philippians is simply a letter of thanksgiving that the Apostle Paul wrote from his prison cell in Rome to a small group of Christians in Philippi who had remembered and affirmed him. This same Apostle Paul reminded the Romans and all of us that we are to *"rejoice with those who rejoice; mourn with those who mourn."* (Romans 12:15)

All of us have been created equal in the sense that all of us have our hidden scars. In light of this, it is not surprising that Ian MacLauren wrote "Be kind to one another, for most people you meet in life are facing very difficult battles."

Sometimes we tend to forget that *"cour"* in the word *"courage"* means *"heart."* To *"encourage"* or *"affirm"* someone means to *"put heart into."* Likewise, to *"discourage"* someone means to *"take the heart out."*

Let us become more sensitive to offering words of affirmation, praise and thanksgiving for those around us. Perhaps there is someone near you today that needs a simple, sincere word of encouragement. You may be the only one who is able to *"put heart into"* the life of that individual!

An Unusual Birdie!

Bishop Paul A. Duffey and I were playing golf together at the Montgomery Country Club when I experienced one of the most unbelievable events of my life. When I teed off on the 16th hole, my drive *"right down the middle"* hit a bird, cut the bird's head off, and fell to the ground. The good Bishop and I walked out into the center of the fairway, and there was the bird's head lying three feet from the body. Being a lover of nature, and more especially of birds, I was somewhat shook up. Even though I had played an excellent round of golf for me up to that point, I proceeded to hit my second shot into the trees, then into the sand trap, and across the green before I finally made it to the hole. I really became unglued!

Sometimes when we are sailing smoothly along in life, some unforeseen obstacle comes from out of the middle of nowhere, knocks us down, and overwhelms our concentration. We lose our grip on life and for a period of time, our lives are in disarray. It may be an unfavorable diagnosis from a physician, a car accident, a broken hip, a heart attack, or a failed marriage.

When these unforeseen things come our way, there are different responses that we can make. We can drown ourselves in self-pity. We can repress our feelings and go into a shell. However, we can allow our interruptions to become stepping stones rather than stumbling blocks. Whatever unexpected interruptions come into our lives, we need to hear once again those words that the Apostle Paul wrote to the Romans, "*And we know that in all things God works for the good of those who love him, who have been called according to his purpose.*" (Romans 8:28)

I love the words of the saint, "Thou hast broken my dreams, but only that I might learn to think in Thy broad day. Thou hast put aside my plans, but only that I might open my eyes to the depth and clearness of Thy plan for me."

I have never had a hole-in-one, but I have experienced an unusual "birdie!"

A Miracle at Willow Point

I shall never forget the time that George Thompson, Jr., invited Jeff Davis, Paul Duffey and me to join him for a wonderful golf outing at Willow Point. It was a gorgeous day, not a cloud in the sky, and little did I anticipate what a miraculous thing might happen on such a beautiful morning. George made the decision that he and I would play Jeff and Paul, but little did he realize that Jeff Davis would par the first several holes and we would find ourselves playing catch-up all day. No one who has ever watched me play golf would accuse me of neglecting my "church work" for golf, and once again at Willow Point, I was struggling.

However, when we came to the 16th hole and I found myself 185 yards away on the par 4, I could see the top of the flag, but not the hole, because of the rise in the fairway. I closed my eyes and hit my second shot toward the green. George, my partner, remarked, "That ball is headed straight toward the pin." However, when the four of us got down to the green, George, Jeff, and Paul expressed no confidence at all that my ball might be in the hole! They began their normal search for my ball. When they could not find it in the sand traps, they started looking between the rocks behind the green. When they could not find my ball amid the rocks, they began to look in the water at the edge of Lake Martin. After several minutes of searching in vain where they thought my ball surely must be, Paul Duffey walked over to the hole, looked down, and with a surprised look on his face, said, "Here it is in the hole!" It was the first eagle I had ever scored. Needless to say, the score on that hole did not resemble my scores on any other holes that day. When the golf round was completed, I became amused over the total lack of confidence that the threesome had that my ball could possibly be anywhere near the hole, much less in it.

In a more serious vein, I share that story with you to simply remind you that the instilling of confidence in the life of a child is one of the greatest things a father can do! Children have a way of "living up" or "living down" to a parent's expectations. Deborah Phillips, in her book *How To Give Your Child A Great Self-Image* writes, "Four specific compliments a day that are genuine, specific, and given intermittently can change a child's whole life. A child who is repeatedly called 'dumb' or 'bad' will behave in such a way that justifies the parent's description. However, if a child lives with encouragement, that child learns confidence and will gain a great self-image."

Is there a child in your midst that needs to hear some words of encouragement that might lead toward confidence and a greater self-image? There is no greater time to offer a word of affirmation or encouragement than today!

Biscuits Baseball and Bill Veeck

The Montgomery *Biscuits* have their home opener scheduled this weekend in their sparkling new stadium at the riverfront, and I have been asked to throw out the first pitch for the Sunday afternoon game with Huntsville. While trying to decide between a fastball and slider, I have been reflecting upon a couple of statements made by Tom Dickson, the owner of the Montgomery *Biscuits*. Tom claims that the whole atmosphere for this new Class AA baseball team in Montgomery will be that of creating family entertainment. He also claims that research has shown that over half the persons who leave minor league baseball games do not even know the score!

As I read about Tom Dickson and all of his exciting promotions planned for the Montgomery *Biscuits*, I am reminded of Bill Veeck, the most imaginative promoter in all of major league baseball history. He would do anything to draw a crowd during his stints with the Cleveland Indians, St. Louis Browns, and Chicago White Sox between 1946 and 1980. He was the first owner to have an exploding scoreboard. In his most interesting promotional stunt (on August 19, 1951) Veeck sent Eddie Gaedel, a 3'7" midget, to bat. Wearing the number "1/8," Gaedel walked on four straight pitches! On a "Grandstand Managers' Day," Veeck signed Satchel Paige of Mobile as the

163

oldest rookie (42) in the history of Major League Baseball. He reactivated Minnie Minoso at 54 so that Minoso could say that he had played five decades. He was credited with planting ivy at Wrigley Field and starting the tradition of Harry Caray singing "Take Me Out to the Ballgame" during the seventh inning stretch.

When the Cleveland Indians got off to a horrendous start in 1949, it was Bill Veeck who came up with the creative idea of a "second opening day" on May 17, 1949. On this "second opening day," with a full slate of opening day ceremonies done a second time, the home standing Cleveland Indians went out and beat the Chicago White Sox, 4-0.

Whenever I read about Bill Veeck's "Second Opening Day," I am reminded that all of us at one time or another need a "second chance." One of the most exciting things about the Christian faith is that Christianity is the greatest religion of the "new" that ever came to existence. The Apostle wrote to the Corinthians, *". . . if anyone is in Christ, he is a new creation; the old has gone, the new has come!"* (Second Corinthians 5:17) With springtime bursting out all around us bringing newness of life, let us be reminded that each of us can experience a new start in life as well!

Winners and Losers

I shall never forget Stan White! When I last saw him lying flat on his back on the artificial turf at Legion Field in Birmingham on November 26, 1992, he was writhing in pain from a separated shoulder. One of Alabama's defensive ends, John Copeland, had just administered a bone-crushing tackle late in the game, and this junior from Birmingham was carried off the field to UAB for surgery. Stan White was a symbol of ignominious defeat as a sellout crowd of 83,091 and a national television audience looked on. His Auburn Tigers had not only lost to Alabama, but they had been shut out 17-0, gaining only twenty yards rushing and 119 yards passing. Alabama went on to win the National Championship by beating Miami 34-13 on New Year's Day.

While Stan White was undergoing shoulder surgery and recuperating at UAB Hospital, there were sportswriters and fans everywhere who suggested that it would be best if he "hung up his cleats" and did not return for his senior year at Auburn. After all, his team had struggled through a difficult season, finishing with a 5-5-1 record.

Stan White not only returned to Auburn for his senior year, but he led his Auburn Tigers to an 11-0 record, truly a Cinderella season that was capped off with a 22-14 victory over Alabama in Jordan-Hare Stadium. That remarkable undefeated

165

season also included a great victory over Florida 38-35, as well as a victory over Georgia 42-28. He set a career passing record at Auburn of 8,016 yards, breaking Heisman Trophy winner Pat Sullivan's record of 6,284 yards. Stan White was named the "Most Valuable Player" in the Senior Bowl. He was also named "All SEC."

What is the message of all of this? Sometimes when the Alabama-Auburn game looms larger than life, we need to remember that the *real winners* are those who, like Stan White, can rise from the ashes of defeat and through great determination and perseverance later celebrate a day of triumph. The *real winners* are those who build their lives on the firm foundation of Jesus Christ and ultimately experience victory in life whatever the final score of a football game might be. There is great truth in the old adage, "God does not settle all of his accounts in October," or even November!

Arnold Palmer Shares
Words of Wisdom!

On a brief visit to Wake Forest University in Winston-Salem, North Carolina, I noticed on campus a sign announcing that Arnold Palmer, one of their famous alums, would be delivering their commencement address. I was curiously interested in what this famous golfer would say to the graduates. I later obtained a copy of Arnold Palmer's address that I wanted to pass along to our graduates.

I left my small hometown of Latrobe, Pennsylvania, and the modest home of a country club pro to begin my college education at old Wake Forest College. I was able to do so because of a man by the name of Jim Weaver who thought enough of my abilities as a young golfer to give me a scholarship. You might wonder how somebody my age, whose greatest success came many years ago, can still be in tune with what works in a world that has changed so very much in my lifetime. Certainly, there are many things that I cannot comprehend, but there are still the absolutes that transcend place and time.

1. Hard work will always yield positive results.
2. Be fully aware of the world around you.

3. Act purposely on your strongest perceptions, and then have no regrets.

Bill Gates once said on a similar occasion, 'Life is not fair. Get used to it. The world won't care about your self-esteem. The world will expect you to accomplish something before you feel good about yourself. If you mess up, don't whine about your mistakes. Learn from them. Life is not divided into semesters. You don't get summers off, and few employers are interested in helping you find yourself. Do that on your own time!'

You must know that many adults of my generation despair of your generation. All too often in my primary field of endeavor — sports — the headlines go to the players who defy authority and misbehave on and off the field, players who showboat and show up others. Instead, those who should be recognized more often are the fine athletes who are also fine citizens and role models for the youngsters following in their footsteps.

We must continue to emphasize courtesy, integrity, and compassion. We must maintain the traditions that have made America the greatest country in the world…I appeal to you to try to restore a kinder and gentler atmosphere to this world of ours.

Greed should not be our goal. If we continue to tolerate cheating, stealing, lying and violence, we will be on a path to self-destruction. Only through an all-out effort to get back to the basic values and virtues of humanity can we give future generations the quality of life our forefathers worked and sacrificed for to give us the standards of life we now enjoy in our time.

Family, friends, neighbors, home, church, and community used to be vitally important to most Americans. Perhaps it is time to return to some of those core values.

You will soon be assuming parental roles, and I urge you to accept the responsibility that goes with it. Be the kind of parents who teach your children the basic traits and habits that make good citizens and good human beings. Teach them the common courtesies, good manners, politeness and standards of behavior that will make each and every one of you proud. So, please, go forth from your college careers armed with a determination to truly make our world a better place to live. Tomorrow belongs to you!

Chapter Six

Memories of Patriotism

Patriotism

I love the United States of America, "the land of the free and the home of the brave." I love the Black Belt of Alabama, the sandy beaches of northwest Florida, the red hills of Georgia, the fertile delta of the Mississippi, the wheat lands of Kansas, the black hills of North Dakota, the bluegrass of Kentucky, the Shenandoah Valley of Virginia, the great Smoky Mountains of North Carolina, the majestic Rockies of Colorado, the magnificent glaciers of Alaska, the deep blue seas of Hawaii, and the redwood forests of California.

I love the heroes of American history — Paul Revere and Patrick Henry, Daniel Boone and David Crockett.

I am one of those old-fashioned patriots who gets emotional merely listening to the playing of "The National Anthem" or the singing of "God Bless America."

Yet I must always remind myself as one who dearly loves my country that genuine patriotism is found in those who worship only God and nurture America.

Worship love is that uncritical devotion that is appropriate only to God, the already perfect. To worship anything or anyone other than God is to invite disaster and disappointment. There are persons who worship the United

States and all of its leaders. They are never able to see any imperfection. They have allowed this country to be their God. America is their religion.

Nurture love is the kind of love that patriots offer. It is a kind of love that facilitates growing and maturing. Nurture love is what America needs from those who love her most. Nurture love is the ability to rejoice over those parts of the country that are wonderful and good, while at the same time trying to change those things which are not so good. Nurture love is daring to admit that our country and our policies are not always right, but refusing to renounce our citizenship when we see something is wrong. Nurture love is refusing to say, "America: Love It or Leave It," but rather, "America: Love It and Change It." Real patriots are those who worship God and nurture America. In this spirit, let us express our greatest sense of patriotism!

Remembering My Oldest Brother, Joe

My oldest brother, Joe, died on July 23, 2006. Although I grieve over his loss and already miss him greatly, his death following a lengthy illness came as a welcomed release. I take great comfort today in knowing that he is now in the nearer presence of God.

There is something special about an older brother. Joe was one of those rare individuals who was *always* there to offer brotherly advice. Since he was *always* there from the time that I was born, his death has served as a startling reminder of my own mortality.

Joe was a typical firstborn—super-achiever, decision-maker, smart, successful. In school, he always finished at the top of his class. It seems like only yesterday that we loaded up our one-family car in Emelle, only 3 miles from the Mississippi line, rode across central Alabama to take Joe to Alabama Polytechnic Institute. We drove along old Highway 80 through the heart of towns like Livingston, Coatopa, Demopolis, Faunsdale, Gallion, Uniontown, Marion Junction, Selma, Montgomery, Tuskegee, and into the "Loveliest Village on the Plains." Joe had no car, and we left him there with a suitcase, a few clothes, and all of his earthly belongings. There was no task too menial for Joe as he worked his way through college.

While at Auburn, he met and fell in love with Eleanor Allen from Demopolis. They were married, and God blessed them with five sons—Frank, Allen, Bryan, Danny, and Jeff. When Joe graduated with honors from Auburn, he embarked upon a distinguished career in the United States Air Force. Joe's family, like all military families, made great sacrifices as they moved with him to military bases wherever he was assigned. They lived in places all across our nation. His family remained in the States, of course, while he was flying over 200 missions in Vietnam. One of his most interesting assignments was to NASA out in Houston. He was chosen to serve as the coordinator of astronaut training activities and debriefing officer for a couple of Gemini flights. When Joe was pictured in *Life* magazine, debriefing the astronauts on the ship USS *Wasp*, my mother bought up all of the *Life* magazines in rural west Alabama because she was so proud of her oldest son.

When Joe completed his military career, he came back home to his native soil in west Alabama, and ran for public office. He was elected each time that he ran as tax assessor of Sumter County and later Mayor of York. When his health began to fail, he gave up his position as Mayor of York, and he and Eleanor moved to Demopolis. One of the most admirable things that Joe did during the last years of his life was to take such good care of every need for my dear mother.

174

I will be going to Arlington National Cemetery on September 21, 2006, to officiate at the service where Joe's earthly remains will be laid to rest. There will be an honor guard, a military band, and beautiful white horses pulling a caisson, along with active members of the United States Air Force standing at attention, holding a draped flag over his grave. I will read a few verses of Scripture, along with the poem "High Flight" that his wife Eleanor has requested. I have decided not to focus my remarks on his significant achievements in life, but rather to simply give thanks to God for Joe, an older brother who was *always* there!

Freedom is Never Free!

I have always loved July 4th celebrations, and down through the years I have been fascinated in reading the stories of the fifty-six persons who signed our Declaration of Independence. Only one was a clergyman, while twenty-nine were either lawyers or judges. There were nine farmers, nine merchants, three physicians, one printer, one iron-master, one political leader, one surveyor, and one soldier. The oldest signer was Benjamin Franklin, who was seventy. Two of the signers, Thomas Lynch, Jr., and Edward Rutledge were twenty-six. Of the fifty-six who signed our Declaration of Independence, nine died in the Revolutionary War. Five were captured and executed by the British. The homes of twelve of them were ransacked and burned. I have always found it interesting that two of the most famous men who signed the Declaration of Independence, Thomas Jefferson and John Adams, died fifty years later on July 4, 1826.

Whenever we pause to celebrate our nation's independence, we must remember that freedom is never free, but rather freedom has been bought with a terrible price! There is an inscription over the gate to the allied cemetery in Assam, in northeast India, that reads "Tell them that we gave our *todays* for their *tomorrows.*"

I have stood at the Pearl Harbor Memorial and looked down into the beautiful blue waters off the shore of Hawaii. Underneath my feet, just below the water's surface, I could see the USS *Arizona* in which 1,177 American servicemen, many of whom were teenagers, are entombed. One cannot think of those 1,177 young men who gave their very lives without being mindful of the millions of courageous men and women who fought for our nation's freedom. We must not forget those sacrificial servants who gave their last ounce of devotion that we might enjoy all of our freedoms of life today. As we celebrate Independence Day, may we also remember the words of the hymn.

In the beauty of the lilies,
Christ was born across the sea,
With a glory in His bosom
that transfigures you and me.
As He died to make men holy,
let us die to make men free,
While God is marching on.

God is With Us!

One of the most inspiring memorials that I have ever seen is the Vietnam Veterans Memorial in Washington, D. C. The black granite wall is startling in its simplicity and very moving in its impact. The names of those who died in the Vietnam War are etched into that seemingly endless black granite wall in letters of gold.

When the memorial was nearing completion in 1982, a very strange thing happened. Family members who had lost their loved ones in Vietnam began to gather at the construction site from all across America. When construction workers allowed them inside the construction site, the visitors would walk along that stark, black, granite wall. They would reach out and touch a name that was etched in the granite in gold.

One writer described it by saying, "It was almost as if the stone were alive! The touches were gentle, filled with feeling."

Maya Lin, the twenty-year-old architectural student at Yale University whose design for the memorial won the national competition, recalled the very first time she made it to the memorial that she designed. She said, "Like so many others, I searched out a name, the name of a friend's father. As I reached out and touched that name, I cried."

178

If you visit the Vietnam Veterans Memorial today, you will be moved by the number of wives and husbands, fathers and mothers, sisters and brothers, sons and daughters, aunts and uncles, nephews and nieces, and comrades from all across our nation who come to that memorial to touch a name that is etched into the black granite wall.

Why is this true? It is simply because that memorial provides a moment of identification, a presence, a moment of sharing, when one life just for a moment touches another.

That, my friends, is the story of the miracle of the incarnation, God's identification with us in the Babe that was born in Bethlehem's manger. Dietrich Bonhoeffer described God's coming to earth in human flesh as "The Beyond in the Midst of Life."

The writer of Matthew's gospel spoke of the incarnation when he said, ". . . *and they will call him Immanuel"— which means, "God with us."* (Matthew 1:23)

In all of our humanness and imperfections, God comes to us in the presence of Jesus Christ to walk beside us, to make His presence known to us, and to let us know that he identifies with us in all of our struggles in life.

Whatever problems you might be facing this week, remember one thing—*God is with us!*

Remembering
September 11, 2001:
The Worst and the Best

September 11, 2001, will be etched in my mind for the rest of my life! What began as such a beautiful day with lots of sunshine was quickly transformed into one of the darkest days in America's history. In the blink of an eye our lives were changed forever. C. S. Lewis once wrote, "God whispers to us in our pleasures. He speaks to us in our conscience, and He shouts to us in our pain. " Following September 11, I think that God shouted a message that I shall not soon forget about the worst and best of humankind. The dastardly deeds of terrorists were vivid reminders of the worst examples of man's inhumanity to man. These terrorists who perpetrated these senseless acts left hatred as their very last message.

However, we must not overlook the fact that following September 11, we saw the very best in the hearts of men and women across our nation. The heroic efforts of police officers, firefighters, and rescue teams that paid the supreme sacrifice seeking to rescue persons that they had never met, but each precious in the eyes of God, are not easily forgotten. Within minutes after the tragedy, people lined up for blocks at blood banks all across our nation to have their own blood flow into the veins of those critically injured. Southerners and Yankees, black and white, rich and poor, educated and uneducated, CEOs and unskilled laborers suddenly became one in a great outpouring of love. Groups that are often divided were united in a common cause. Adults, youth, and children overflowed sanctuaries all across America to participate in worship services and prayer vigils for the victims and their families.

While the terrorists were obviously shouting their last words of hate from the cockpit of the hijacked airlines during the last minutes of their lives, it is highly significant that passengers on those very same planes were using their telephones to call their mothers, fathers, wives, husbands, sons and daughters to say a last *"I love you!"*

Will Sledge, grandson of our own George and Anne Thompson, was seated in his office on the 51st floor of the World Trade Center when the first plane crashed into the building. He was fortunate enough to escape. In an e-mail that he wrote to his grandparents, George and Anne, Will included these words,

> I cannot tell you how profound this experience has been on me. This event has really made me focus on a few things, namely, my family. I realize now that I am extremely lucky to have my life. After getting out of that building and seeing the horror all around, I can honestly say, 'God can give no one a bigger

wakeup call.' What I want to let everyone know is that I love all of you more than I can express in words. You mean so much to me, and I know that sometimes we all take that love for granted. We expect everyone to be there the next time we pick up the phone. As I have learned, this may not always be the case. I have been thanking the Lord for sparing me, and I hope that I can use this experience to grow stronger in my life. I ask my family and friends to pray for the families who have lost loved ones and I want you to keep them in your hearts. May we unite to overcome this disaster. I love you all very much!

We as Christians must never forget that when man had done his worst, God did His best! That is why during the most difficult days of life, I always choose to focus on the cross.

Augusta Powell Forrest Laid to Rest in Arlington National Cemetery

One of the most unforgettable experiences of my life took place on December 20, 2004, when I officiated at the funeral service of Augusta Powell Forrest at the Arlington National Cemetery, located just across the Potomac River from Washington, D.C. Augusta had attained the rank of Lieutenant Commander in the United States Navy during World War II, serving as a Chief Nurse at Base Hospital Number 12 in southern England. It was to that hospital that the critically wounded on D-Day were evacuated.

Augusta was buried alongside 265,000 other persons who had faithfully served our nation. As we entered Arlington National Cemetery, one of the first things I noticed was that the flags are flown at half-staff from a half hour before the first funeral until a half hour after the last funeral each day. Approximately twenty-two funerals are conducted there each day, excluding weekends. As we drove by the Tomb of the Unknowns, I was reminded that the tomb has been faithfully guarded for twenty-four hours a day, 365 days a year, since the Third United States Infantry began guarding the Tomb on April 6, 1948.

Augusta's funeral at Arlington, like all others, was conducted with such great respect and dignity. A representative of the Secretary of the Navy, Lady Arlington, accompanied me in advance to the site where Augusta's service was to be held. There I saw eight Navy pallbearers, standing at attention in freezing weather, waiting for the family members and friends to arrive. As the Navy pallbearers lifted the casket from the hearse and marched to the graveside, they did so with short steps in great precision. During the whole service, the Navy pallbearers held an unfurled flag over the casket. When I pronounced the benediction, there were seven members of the Navy that gave a twenty-one gun salute. Then from the distance, I could hear the melody of "Amazing Grace," those words I know so well, being played on a bagpipe.

The service closed with a Navy officer kneeling before James, Augusta's faithful husband of fifty-six years, and presenting him the flag. The Navy officer looked into the eyes of James and said, "This flag is presented on behalf of a grateful nation as a token of our appreciation for the honorable and faithful service rendered by your loved one."

I must confess that tears came into my eyes. As I walked away, I was reminded once again that *"freedom is never free; it was bought with a terrible price."*

184

The Greatest Generation

I have never cried at any commencement service except the one that I attended on May 16, 2005, at Emory University. Tom Brokaw, the famous anchor for NBC-TV, was the commencement speaker. It was not surprising that he chose at the close of his speech to talk about "The Greatest Generation." You may recall that in preparation for a documentary on D-Day, Brokaw made a visit to Normandy. As he walked along the beaches with American veterans, Brokaw listened to their stories and was deeply moved by all that they had done. When he gazed at the American cemetery overlooking Omaha Beach in Normandy, he saw 9,368 white marble headstones in long, even lines across the manicured fields of dark green, each headstone marking the death of a brave young American. When Brokaw came back home to America, he was convinced beyond a shadow of a doubt that these men and women who were veterans of World War II comprised the greatest generation that ever lived. These closing words of Tom Brokaw's commencement address at Emory brought tears to my eyes.

Sixty years ago this summer, another generation of young Americans were returning home to restart their lives after more than a dozen years of brutal depravation, sacrifice, separation, death, and grievous wounds. These young Americans had come of age in the Great Depression, when life was about

185

depravation and sharing. Children dropped out of school in the eighth grade, not to buy a pair of sneakers but to put food on the table, or to pay for medical care for their mothers and fathers. Ragged bands of hungry men rode the rails looking for any kind of work. Banks failed, and hope had to be renewed every 24 hours. Just as these young people your age were beginning to emerge from those dark and difficult days, they were summoned to the great cause of defeating Nazi Germany.

Many farm kids who had never seen the ocean signed up for the Navy. Young daredevils who were fascinated by the new frontiers of flight volunteered for pilot training. When they answered that call they were forced to fight their way across North Africa, the deadly beaches of France and Italy, the freezing winters of Europe, and the searing heat of the little known islands of the South Pacific.

Everywhere in America, everyone joined in making some kind of sacrifice. At home, farmers grew more food and civilians ate less so that soldiers could be well fed. Young wives and children did not see their husbands or fathers or hear from them for months at a time, if ever again. Women left the house and put on overalls and work boots and hard hats and carried lunchboxes to the assembly lines.

When the war was over, this generation of Americans your age returned to their homes. They went to college in record numbers, and they married in record numbers. They did something that had never been done in the history of warfare. They rebuilt their enemies. They gave us great institutions like the one that you enjoy here today. They gave us no less than the lives that we have in America now. They did not lay down their arms and say as they could have, 'I've done my share.' Instead they came home and became immersed in their communities and their churches and their schools. They ran for political office. They formed service clubs, and they never gave up on the idea of common cause and their role in it. Some are here today in their distinctive gold robes. They are looking on with pride and humility at the promise of your generation—the opportunities available to you that would have been unimaginable to them. I call them *The Greatest Generation*. They asked so little of us, and yet we owe so much to them. Remember them as you leave here today!

Let us pause this Independence Day and give thanks to God for *The Greatest Generation*!

Chapter Seven

Memories of Laughter

A Rendezvous with a Squirrel!

Brenda and I awoke early one morning and heard a squirrel in the attic. When we walked out into the backyard, we discovered that the squirrel had gnawed a hole through a dormer to get inside. I quickly called Buddy Snipes and asked him to stop by and replace the board with the hole in it. Buddy was very prompt in his response in replacing and painting the board. The very next night, though, the squirrel gnawed another hole in the very same spot and again took residence in the attic.

Needless to say, if it had been my boyhood home, I would have quickly taken matters into my own hands, pulled out my 410, and promptly killed the squirrel. However, I was aware that the city ordinances prevented such drastic action, so I decided that I would resort to less violent means of getting rid of the culprit. One of our wise church members informed Brenda that the scent of mothballs would do the trick! Brenda stopped by the store, purchased some fresh mothballs, and threw them like hand grenades into the far reaches of our attic.

However, matters grew worse. When we prepared to go to bed that rainy night, we found that the smell of the mothballs descended through the vents into our bedroom. We became the two victimized by the sharp odor while the squirrel peacefully slept outside.

It was then that I called Brad Norris. He let me borrow his antique squirrel trap. I loaded it down with pecans and peanuts, but there was one great problem. The trap door did not release, and the squirrel ate all of the nuts without leaving a crumb. I then went over to Moody Hardware and bought a new squirrel cage for $42.11. By then, my investment to get rid of the squirrel had escalated, with the cost of the cage in addition to previously purchased mothballs, peanuts, and pecans.

There was finally a break in this ordeal! I put my loaded squirrel trap at the base of the tree in my backyard that night and caught the squirrel. When my trauma had finally come to an end after several days, I began to think that there must be some theological application to all of this. It then dawned upon me that sometimes sin, like a sneaky squirrel, can creep in on us very inauspiciously and take up residence within our hearts. Before too many days pass, we wake up and discover that we would have been so much better off if we had only taken drastic action at the beginning. We finally realize that we could have saved so much hurt and heartache if we had only taken immediate action at the outset to eradicate the sin.

By the way, when I caught the squirrel, I released him at the base of a big oak tree in the front yard of one of our wise church members who recommended the mothballs!

My Last Visit to a Beauty Shop!

As a pastor I get to know many wonderful people in all walks of life. A hair stylist came to me several years ago and asked if I would officiate at her wedding. During our conversation, she encouraged me to stop by her beauty shop sometime and let her cut my hair. Although I felt somewhat uneasy about this idea, I was later encouraged when I learned that she cut the hair of several other men in Montgomery. Several months passed before I mustered up enough courage to call her beauty shop and ask if I could drop by for the very last appointment on a Friday afternoon. When I entered the front door, I received a few stares. However, I felt if my male friends could put up with that kind of body language abuse, so could I for a few minutes. She quickly cut my hair, and I was on my way.

This same hair stylist then made a decision to move to a larger beauty shop that had wide-open seating for all of its customers. This made it even more difficult for me to get up enough nerve to walk into that arena of staring women. However, I once again mustered enough nerve to give it a try.

191

The only appointment available when I called was 10:00 a.m. No last appointment in the afternoon this time. When I walked into the beauty shop, it appeared that half of the women seated in the open area were members of our church.

When the hair stylist insisted on washing my hair before cutting it, I raised up just in time to get a strange look from one of the wet-haired, female members of our church sitting next to me. I covered my face with a towel while I waited for my name to be called for a haircut.

While I anxiously waited, I peeped out from under my towel. I looked in the face of another church member seated on the other side of me. She looked as though she was preparing for a lift-off to Mars. She had what appeared to be a whole roll of tin foil in layers around her head. The rolls of tin foil stood out like antennas, which appeared as though she was picking up signals from outer space.

Although she did not say a word, she looked the other way with an embarrassed look on her face as if to say, "What in the world are you doing in here?"

When I glanced across the room again my eyes fixed on another church member who had what appeared to be "Mississippi mud" around her hairline. When she looked in my direction it was very evident she wished that I were somewhere else.

192

I breathed a silent prayer to God in which I said that if He would help me through that one appointment, I promised that I would never, never go back to another beauty shop.

I share that story with you simply to say that all of us like to go to places where we feel warmly welcomed and affirmed. We stay away from those places where we feel out of place. In light of this, the church, as the body of Christ, should always embody the spirit of Jesus Christ that goes the extra mile in making people feel welcome. The church, at its very best, is a place where we heed the Biblical admonition to "practice hospitality."

Let us seek out those who feel uncomfortable and welcome them into our midst. In the meantime, I promise to stay out of beauty shops!

A True Detective Story

     Sitting in my church office one morning I received a telephone call from Corporal John Gallops, a detective with the Montgomery City Police Department. He asked if I could come down immediately to the police headquarters on North Ripley Street. I sensed from the sound of his voice that something was really wrong. From the time that I got into my car at the church until the time I arrived at the police headquarters, I thought of everything that I had done wrong in my lifetime. I especially remembered when I was a little boy, I brought home a towel from a hotel. My mother found it in my suitcase and made me go to the post office at 8:00 o'clock in the morning and mail it back with a letter of apology.

     When I reached the police headquarters, I entered through the back door. I had to push the security button for the man at the front desk to open the locked door. When I told the man at the desk that I was there to see Detective Gallops, I was escorted up a flight of stairs through a second set of locked doors to Detective Gallops' office where I met him for the first time. I sat down across the desk of Detective Gallops and asked, "What's going on?"

     "I can't tell you right now," the detective announced "I must read you your Miranda rights, have you sign some papers, and then we will proceed. You are a suspect in a crime."

He placed in front of me a payroll check from Baptist Home Services made out to me for $685.00. He asked me if I recognized it, and I said "*No.*" He then turned it over and asked if the endorsement on the back was my signature and I said "*No.*"

I learned that someone had stolen a payroll check from Baptist Home Services, typed in my name as payee, and cashed it at a local pawn shop. The detective released me on my own recognizance and I drove back to the church.

I could visualize a headline in the *Montgomery Advertiser* which read "Methodist Preacher Steals from Baptist and Cashes Check at Local Pawn Shop.*"*

The story does not end there.

A few days later, Detective Gallops called me a second time and said "I'm getting married in a couple of weeks, and I would like for you to come and 'read me my rights' as you officiate at my wedding."

On a lovely Saturday afternoon, I had the joy of standing before Detective Gallops and his bride Deborah reminding him of the sacred vows to God that should not be broken. I read these familiar words:

Marriage is an honorable estate, instituted by God. It is not to be entered into unadvisedly, but reverently, discreetly, and in the fear of God. If these solemn vows are kept inviolate, as God's word demands, and if steadfastly you endeavor to do the will of your heavenly Father, God will bless your marriage, will grant you fulfillment in it, and will establish your home in peace.

I pronounced a benediction or blessing to the good detective and his bride. As I drove back home, I could not help but rejoice that all of the mysteries had been solved and everyone went home happy.

Jerry Clower

I was a great fan of Jerry Clower! I found it somewhat refreshing that he was unapologetically Christian in the entertainment world. Several years ago, I was listening to the halftime show of an Auburn University basketball game from the SEC Tournament being played in Rupp Arena in Lexington, Kentucky.

During the intermission the Auburn announcer interviewed Jerry Clower, and Jerry gave credit to two Alabamians for launching his career as a professional entertainer. Of the millions of Alabamians, I thought it was interesting that both men he named as encouraging him to become a comedian were faithful members of our First United Methodist Church of Montgomery — Nick Harris and Ham Wilson, Sr.

One of my favorite Jerry Clower stories was the one he told about the woman in Amity County, Mississippi. She lived near a construction site where workers were in the process of putting a tar roof on a building near her house.

The lady had sixteen children or *"young'uns"* as Jerry called them. One day she lost one of her children. Her diligent search revealed that this young boy of hers had fallen in a fifty-gallon drum of black roofing tar. She reached down, pulled him out, took a long look at his body covered with tar, and shoved him back into the drum saying, "Boy, it would be a lot easier to have another one than to clean you up!"

I am sure that God must often feel that way about us. Surely we try his patience with our faults and failures. I am sure that God has been tempted to say at times, "*It surely would be easier to start a new one than clean him or her up.*" Yet the good news of Jesus Christ is the good news that God prefers to clean us up rather than replace us.

Let us remember those words found in I John 1:9 "*If we confess our sins, he is faithful and just and will forgive us our sins and purify us from all unrighteousness.*"

Heaven

Tom Allison, one of our most faithful members, had a wonderful sense of humor. After graduating from Huntingdon College, Tom spent a fascinating career as a Special Investigator with the Alcohol, Tobacco, and Firearms Division of the United States Treasury Department.

When he began his career in 1955, a major part of his work with ATF was devoted to the enforcement of liquor laws and tracking down moonshine stills. Out of that experience Tom wrote a delightful book entitled *Moonshine Memories*. Tom dedicates his book to his four grandchildren: Kelsey and Leigh Allison, and Jacob and Matthew Woodham. In the Preface to his book, Tom tells the story of an unforgettable experience with Kelsey, his oldest grandchild.

Kelsey, about three, was visiting in Montgomery, and her mother and father were coming to visit that weekend. This was in the fall of the year and the squirrels were trying to take over the pecan trees in the backyard by adverse possession. That was bad enough, but it was even worse when they started trying to get into the attic. When I saw a squirrel jump from a low limb onto the roof, I eased out into the backyard and shot him with a .22 caliber rifle. Kelsey followed me out into the yard. She wasn't the least bit upset, and I forgot about the incident until Lindsey and

199

Russ arrived on Friday night. Kelsey ran wide-eyed toward her mother shouting, 'Mama, mama, Paw Paw shot a squirrel.'

Lindsey told her, 'Now, Honey, don't worry about that squirrel. That squirrel is in heaven.' Kelsey immediately replied, 'Mama, that 'quirrel's not in heaven. He is out there in the trash can.'

When I read Tom's story of Kelsey, I thought about how confused some of us become when we talk about someone going to heaven. The important thing for us to remember is what Christina Rosetti wrote in her poem *Seek and Find*: "Heaven is the presence of God. "

Jesus said, *"In my Father's house are many rooms; if it were not so, I would have told you. I am going there to prepare a place for you. And if I go and prepare a place for you, I will come back and take you to be with me that you also may be where I am. "*(John 14:2,3) The word "heaven" is used most often to describe the place where the redeemed shall ultimately be in the presence of Jesus Christ. As Kelsey grows older, she will learn that no matter where our earthly remains might be placed, there is an eternal truth in the words of the Psalmist, *"Precious in the sight of the Lord is the death of His saints."* (Psalm 116:15)

For All Golfers

Bishop Bruce Blake tells the story of the golfer who teed off on a water hole and proceeded to hit five balls into the water. The man then slowly placed his iron back into his golf bag, walked up to the edge of the lake, and threw his bags with all of his clubs into the water. The foursome behind him watched in utter amazement as the frustrated golfer then hurriedly walked toward the parking lot to get into his car and drive home.

The foursome behind the frustrated golfer was concerned that the man may have thrown away some very expensive golf clubs, and they paused to observe the man walking to his car, hoping that he might have a change of heart. They were pleased to see that when the frustrated golfer finally reached his car, he seemed to have experienced a change of heart. The man turned around and appeared to be headed back toward the golf course to retrieve his clubs.

The foursome then watched as the frustrated golfer went back down to the edge of the lake, took off his golf shoes, walked out into the lake that was waist deep, pulled a watch out of the golf bag, and then politely proceeded to throw his golf bag with all of his clubs back into the water!

There are many ways that we can respond to the stresses of life, and perhaps serious golf is not the answer! Christian psychologists remind us that we can handle stress more effectively when we establish realistic expectations of ourselves. When we try to live up to some superman / superwoman image, we tend to forget that we are creatures, and not the Creator. We can also respond to the stresses of life more effectively when we find time for God.

The great prophet Isaiah wrote (40:31) ". . . *but those who hope in the Lord will renew their strength. They will soar on wings like eagles; they will run and not grow weary, they will walk and not be faint.*" Isaiah also reminded us (30:15) "*In repentance and rest is your salvation, in quietness and trust is your strength . . ..*"

When we become stressed out in life, we must remember that the word *"anger"* is only one letter short of *"danger."* Let us focus on God who gives us strength to handle every stressful situation of life.

John's Plumbing: We Repair What Your Husband Fixed!

Patrick Quinn and I were riding along Interstate 59 just north of Birmingham when he pointed out to me an interesting sign which read, "John's Plumbing: We Repair What Your Husband Fixed!"

The words on that sign really struck home to me for obvious reasons. Brenda and I have enjoyed a wonderful marriage over the past forty-one years but I am convinced that when I die, the next time around she would much rather marry someone whose occupation was a plumber or a handyman rather than a minister. I take some small comfort in knowing that I have several friends who are in the same boat.

Interestingly enough, my father was a mechanic, but I have always been "all thumbs" when it comes to making repairs. Brenda holds title to the only toolbox in our home, and down through the years, she has increasingly said, *"I would just rather fix it myself!"*

The sign for "John's Plumbing" served as a reminder to me of the Biblical truth that each of us has been blessed with unique gifts.

When the Apostle Paul wrote his letter to the Ephesians, he emphasized that there is a variety of spiritual gifts.

Some can teach. Others can preach or ring hand bells. Some can cook or serve. Some can encourage. Others can fix!

By the way, we have a dripping faucet over our sink. If someone could help Brenda with this plumbing problem, great will be your reward in heaven!

Chapter Eight

Memories of Inspiration

When You Care Enough to Send the Very Best

While attending a conference in Kansas City, Missouri, I visited the Hallmark Card International Headquarters. There were several things that the guide shared with our group that intrigued me:

1. Joyce C. Hall, the man who founded Hallmark Cards, came from a devout Methodist family. He was born on August 29, 1891, in the small town of David City, Nebraska.

2. He was named after a Methodist bishop, Isaac W. Joyce, who happened to be visiting in the small town of David City when Joyce C. Hall was born.

3. Joyce C. Hall bought a one-way bus ticket in 1910 from David City, Nebraska, to Kansas City, and it was there that he founded Hallmark Cards.

4. During the tragic events of September 11, 2001, there was a great increase in the sale of Hallmark Cards. People who oftentimes struggle to communicate their deepest feelings resort to the use of cards.

5. The slogan of Hallmark Cards, "When You Care Enough to Send the Very Best," began in 1944 in the midst of World War II. It became one of the most enduring advertising slogans in history.

6. The most popular Hallmark greeting card continued through all of the years has been the one with purple pansies and three simple words, "Thinking of you!"

7. There are 34,000,000 Mother's Day cards mailed each year, and only 40% of those by sons and daughters.

8. One of the most popular quotes on a Hallmark Card down through the years has been "When you get to the end of your rope, tie a knot and hang on!"

9. One of the greatest increases in sales among Father's Day cards has been a new Hallmark Card that conveys a message from the family dog to the father of the house.

10. The most popular poem on a Hallmark Card down through the years has been Edgar Guest's poem "Friends."

> I'd like to be the sort of friend
> > that you have been to me,
>
> I'd like to be the help
> > you are always glad to be.

I'd like to mean as much to you
   every minute of the day,

As you have meant, good friend of mine,
   to me along the way.

And this is just to wish
   that I could somehow repay

A portion of the gladness
   that you have strewn along the way.

For could I have one wish today,
   this only would it be,

I'd like to be the sort of friend
   that you have been to me!

Living One Day at a Time

I love the story of the little boy who was walking through his neighborhood selling magazines for his school. When he came to the home of a very elderly gentleman, the little boy rang the doorbell and patiently waited for someone to answer the door.

When the elderly gentleman finally opened the door, the little boy looked up at him and said, "Sir, would you like to buy a three-year subscription to your favorite magazine?"

The elderly gentleman looked down at the little boy and said, "Son, at my age I don't even buy green bananas."

Perhaps there is a lesson for all of us in that little story. Too many of us spend too much time "subscribing" to things in the future, and we fail to appreciate all of the wonderful things that are happening all around us in the present moment.

Dale Carnegie once said, "The most tragic thing about human beings is that most of us put off living. We dream of some magical rose garden across the horizon, and we fail to enjoy the beautiful roses that are blooming outside our windows today."

Sir William Osler came to America over one hundred years ago to share with Americans his "secret philosophy of life." He claimed that he had discovered happiness only when he had learned to live in "single day compartments of life."

Jesus said, ". . . do not worry about tomorrow. . . . Each day has enough troubles of its own." (Matthew 6:34)

Charlie Brown of "Peanuts" fame said, "I only dread one day at a time."

The Psalmist encouraged us to live one day at a time when he wrote these lines, "This is the day the Lord has made; let us rejoice and be glad in it." (Psalm 118:24)

Don't Make Tragedies of Trifles; Don't Shoot Butterflies with Rifles!

While attending the Southeastern Conference basketball tournament in Memphis, Tennessee, not long ago, I was approached by a man who walked up to me at a concession stand and identified himself as Russell Stutts. He said that he was a member of the Canterbury United Methodist Church in Birmingham and had heard me speak at the Church in the Pines at Lake Martin. He then quoted a little couplet that I had used on that occasion.

> Don't make tragedies of trifles;
> Don't shoot butterflies with rifles!

I was impressed that he had remembered the couplet, but I was even more impressed when he said that he and his wife had repeated those words nearly every morning across the years.

Much of the stress that we experience in life can be traced to our failure to distinguish between the major and minor things of life. We spend far too much time and energy worrying over trivial matters. It is amazing how we fail to discern between the significant and the insignificant.

211

Jesus spoke to the heart of this issue when He said, *"So do not worry. . . . But seek first his kingdom and his righteousness. . . ."* (Matthew 6:31, 33)

Perhaps all of us could live happier lives if we could gain a perspective on our priorities. There will always be mistakes and errors in judgment. There will always be those who will offer criticism or apply subtle pressure. However, in the spirit of Jesus Christ, we should heed the words of the unknown writer:

Don't make tragedies of trifles;
Don't shoot butterflies with rifles!

I Did Not Forget a Single One!

Barbara Wilkerson shared with me the inspiring story of a little boy whose name was Brad. He and his parents had moved into a new neighborhood. Brad was very quiet and shy. When Valentine's Day drew near he told his mother that he wanted to make a valentine for every child in his class. His mother's heart sank. She knew that her son would be hurt in the process, for every afternoon when the kids walked home from school, laughing and talking with one another, Brad trudged along far behind, always at a safe distance.

A week before the Valentine's Day celebration, the mother decided that she would go along with her son's idea, and so she bought him some red and white paper, glue, crayons, and glitter. Brad spent his after-school hours creating thirty-five valentines.

When Valentine's Day finally arrived, Brad was so excited. With his bundle of valentines under his arm, he raced out the front door of his home to get to school before all of his classmates arrived. However, it was a terrible day for his mother. All day long she thought to herself, "This is going to be such a tough day for Brad. I want to do something very special for him when he gets home to ease his pain for I know that he will not get many valentines."

That afternoon when school dismissed she anxiously looked out the window to catch a glimpse of her son. She saw him at a distance, walking far behind a large group of children that were laughing and talking with their bright valentines under their arms. As she had anticipated, her first glimpse of Brad in the far distance was one in which she saw him walking alone. The mother said to herself, "Bless his heart! His arms are empty, and he is about to burst into tears." When Brad walked into the house she said, "Honey, your mother has prepared something very special for you this evening." As he looked up at his mother, she was somewhat startled to see that his face was all aglow. With a broad smile upon his face he marched past her and declared triumphantly, "I did not forget a single one. I did not forget a single one!"

I love that story simply because it reminds us that love is never selfish. Love does not seek its own way. Love is always found in giving, not in getting. Do you remember the lyrics to that great old hymn "Others"?

Lord, help me live from day to day
in such a self-forgetful way
That even when I kneel to pray,
my prayer may be for others.
Others, Lord, yes, others, let this my motto be,
Help me to live for others, that I may live like Thee.

Life's Little Instruction Book

Jackson Brown, Jr., was preparing to send his son Adam off to college several years ago when Jackson thought that he would jot down a few practical suggestions for his son. To his own surprise, Jackson came up with 511.

He offered such suggestions as, "Compliment three people each day. Plant flowers every spring. Never give up on anybody. Praise in public. Criticize in private. Have your children earn and pay for their automobile insurance. Look people in the eye. Write thank you notes promptly. Show respect for military personnel. Learn CPR. Call your mother."

Jackson Brown placed all of his practical suggestions into a notebook. On the day that Jackson helped Adam move into his dormitory for his freshman year, he handed the notebook of practical suggestions to his son as they were standing in the parking lot.

Although Jackson Brown never intended for all of his practical suggestions to be printed, those words of fatherly wisdom were published under the title of *Life's Little Instruction Book*. Millions of copies of that little book have been sold around the world.

Many years ago when the Apostle Paul found himself a prisoner in Rome, he took out his pen and wrote some words of practical advice to the Philippians, "... *conduct yourselves in a manner worthy of the gospel of Christ. . . . Have his mind in you which was also in Christ Jesus. . . . Whatever is true, honorable, just; whatever is pure, lovely, and gracious; if there is any excellence, if there is anything worthy of praise, think about these things."* (Philippians 1:27; 2:5, 4:8)

As many of our high school graduates leave for college, it is important that each of them remembers the practical advice that is found in *God's Instruction Book*!

Things Turn Out for the Best
for Those Who Make the Best of
the Way Things Turn Out

My oldest daughter Stacie kept a quotation on her mirror throughout her high school and college days. It read simply "Things turn out for the best for those who make the best of the way things turn out."

I believe that! My favorite Bible verse through the years has been Romans 8:28: *"And we know that in all things God works for the good of those who love him, who have been called according to his purpose."*

Not everything that happens to us is good. There are so many disappointments in life. Sometimes a change in jobs will initiate a move to a new location, uprooting family members from friends.

Our best-laid plans often go astray, and we are tempted to drown ourselves in self-pity amid the ashes of disappointment.

The Apostle Paul in his letter to the Romans reminds us that God never promised us immunity from the disappointments of life, but He did promise us that every disappointment might be turned into something good.

One of my favorite poets, Robert Browning, came to the close of his life, looked back across the years and said, "I have seen God's hand in a lifetime, and I know it was all for the best!"

Remember this day and every day: "Things turn out for the best for those who make the best of the way things turn out."

Our Unseen Benefactors

One of my favorite Sundays of the year is Palm Sunday! There is something very thrilling to relive that moment long ago when Jesus Christ rode triumphantly into the city of Jerusalem. As we remember that day when children waved their palm branches and shouted their loud "Hosannas," I am always intrigued by one part of the Palm Sunday story that is often overlooked.

Who was the unnamed person in Jerusalem that owned the donkey and made preparations for this significant moment in the life of Jesus? That unnamed individual had a very special role in what happened that day, but he is often overlooked.

That part of the Palm Sunday story serves as a silent reminder that all of us have unseen benefactors that touch our lives in various and sundry ways. There are always benefactors in mothers and fathers, sisters and brothers, aunts and uncles. However, there are also unseen benefactors in caring teachers, faithful friends, and persons that enrich our lives in small and simple ways day by day.

In light of this, someone has developed an interesting quiz:

Name the ten wealthiest persons in the world.

Name the last ten Heisman trophy winners.
Name the last ten winners of the Miss America pageant.
Name ten persons who have won the Nobel Prize.
Name the last ten Academy Award winners for best picture.
Name the last ten winners of the World Series.

With the exception of trivia hounds, none of us remember yesterday's headliners too well. It is rather surprising how quickly we forget. Yet the things mentioned above are not second-rate achievements. These were the best in their chosen fields. However, the applause soon dies. Awards tarnish. So take another quiz!

Think of ten people with whom you enjoy spending your time.
Name ten persons who have taught you something worthwhile.
Name five teachers who have aided your journey through school.
Name five friends who have helped you during a difficult time.

The people who make a difference in our lives are not the ones with the credentials, but rather the ones with the concern. Let us celebrate and give thanks to God for all of the unseen benefactors in our midst that, too often, we take for granted!

Life is What Happens When You Are Making Other Plans

Linda Henley wrote an interesting article in which she began with these thought-provoking words, "Life is what happens to you while you are making other plans."

As she reflected upon her life, she shared the story of how, for many years, she lamented the fact that she had never done much with her life. She had never written a book. She had never become president of a company. She had never been elected to a political office. She had certainly not become rich or famous.

Through the years, she had only seen herself as someone's daughter, someone's wife, someone's mother, and someone's friend. Over and over again through the years she had said to herself, "Someday I will do something meaningful and significant."

Yet that certain "someday" always seemed to be far away in the future, and family needs closer to home were always more pressing.

One day after her husband died, and the children were grown and out on their own, she became somewhat disillusioned by the fact that she had never gotten around to doing anything great with her life.

In a moment of depression, she went out to the cemetery to visit her husband's grave. Reminiscing upon that experience, she wrote:

"I rearranged the flowers and pulled a couple of weeds and talked for a while. Then, as the sun went down, I strolled the deserted cemetery and read the inscriptions on other people's stones...'The Best Mother of All'...'Devoted Dad'... 'Faithful Friend'... 'Parents of Debra, Scott, and Mary Ann'... 'God's Servant for Others.'"

Then she added, "Nowhere in all of that cemetery did I see one single marker that said, 'Successful Banker' or 'Rich and Famous.' Suddenly, as I walked through that cemetery, I had a life-changing experience. I realized something that I had never realized before. When we come to the end of our lives, our lives are reduced to a few simple words on a piece of granite, and those words almost invariably refer to relationships that we have built and the love that we have left behind."

Because of all the wonderful relationships that Linda had enjoyed through the years, she suddenly saw her life as rich and full of meaning. In the rush and hurry of life, let us remember the words of Linda Henley, "Life is what happens when you are making other plans."

In Profound Appreciation of the Boll Weevil

Our own Marjorie Bagwell was crowned the very first "Peanut Queen" in Enterprise, Alabama, in December 1919. The boll weevil monument was unveiled on that occasion.

The story that led to the establishment of this most unusual monument is a part of the interesting history of the State of Alabama. For many, many years, cotton was king in our state. However, when the boll weevil swept through Alabama in 1916, destroying two-thirds of the cotton crop, the cotton farmers around Enterprise, in their hopeless situation, were forced to turn to the planting of peanuts. Little did they realize that in the midst of their loss, the planting of peanuts would bring prosperity to farmers throughout the area.

Out of the ashes of defeat, victory was found. The people who had lost their cotton crops, while finding new prosperity in the planting of peanuts, decided to erect a monument (the only monument in the world that glorifies a pest) to the boll weevil. Today, if you drive through the heart of downtown Enterprise, you will find a goddess on a lighted pedestal holding aloft a giant boll weevil. At the base of the monument is the following inscription:

223

In Profound Appreciation
of the Boll Weevil
and What it Has Done.
As the Herald of Prosperity
This Monument Was Erected
by the Citizens of
Enterprise, Coffee County, Alabama

The unusual story of the boll weevil monument has been retold through the years to illustrate how, in the midst of our greatest disappointments, God is at work bringing newness of life. I guess that is the reason my favorite Bible verse is Romans 8:28: *"And we know that in all things God works for the good of those who love him, who have been called according to his purpose."*

I Didn't Know
How Heavy My Luggage Was
'Til I Stopped Carrying It!

Dr. Robert Schuller is certainly one of the best-known religious broadcasters in America today. Ordained a minister in the Reformed Church, he moved to Garden Grove, California, in 1955, and there he first attracted people by preaching in a local drive-in theater where worshipers listened to him from their parked cars. He later organized the Garden Grove Community Church, and in 1980 his congregation built the Crystal Cathedral. In an interview held with Dr. Schuller a reporter asked, "Of all the sermons that you have preached on television, which one received the greatest response?"

Dr. Schuller replied, "Interestingly enough, it was also the sermon with the longest title, 'I Didn't Know How Heavy My Luggage Was 'Til I Stopped Carrying It!'"

Then Dr. Schuller told the story behind the selection of that title. He said that in most of the places where he traveled, whenever he got off the plane someone would be waiting for him at the airport. Invariably, whenever that designated person would greet him at the airport, that individual would say, "Let me take your bag!"

Dr. Schuller said that for many years, he was very self-conscious and would always respond with words like, "Do I look that old? Do I look that feeble? Do I look that sick? No Thanks! I am strong enough to carry my own bags. "

Dr. Schuller said that one day when he got off the plane and someone greeted him with those familiar words, "Oh, let me take your bag! "he handed the host the heavy suitcase in which he kept several of his books and most important papers. Dr. Schuller claims that it was then that he realized for the very first time that he never knew how heavy his briefcase was until he let go of it and let the man carry it for him. When Dr. Schuller told this story in his televised sermon he asked his audience, "What heavy luggage are you carrying with you this morning that you need to lay down?"

That is a good question for each of us to ask ourselves. "What heavy luggage am I carrying with me today that I need to lay down?" Perhaps it is a terrible sin of the past for which you long to hear a word of forgiveness. Perhaps it is a terrible scar that has come to you as a result of someone who did you wrong. Perhaps it is the heavy luggage of a vengeful spirit. If you are carrying some heavy baggage today, lay it down at the feet of Jesus Christ and experience the joy and happiness that He will bring!

A Lesson Learned from Marvella Bayh

Marvella Bayh, the wife of Senator Birch Bayh of Indiana, lived with cancer for six years before she died. She talked freely about what happens to your perspective on life when you learn the news that you have a terminal illness.

"When I learned the news of my illness life came down to the basics and I was able to put everything in perspective. Things that seemed so important before all of a sudden didn't seem to matter anymore. I discovered suddenly that there are two things in life that are really important: your relationship with God and your relationship with others."

Marvella Bayh was in George Washington Hospital for radiation treatments. She said, "I got to the point where I was feeling rather listless and discouraged and I thought to myself, 'I don't want to go through this. I'm tired of it.' I wanted to give up."

"Our car was easy to identify because of the Senate license plate. One day I came out of the hospital and there was a pencil-scribbled note on the windshield. The note read, 'I see your car parked here every day, Mrs. Bayh. Hang in there. I join others in thinking of you.'"

227

Marvella Bayh concluded, "You don't have to be the President of the United States or a United States Senator to make a difference in people's lives. You can touch people every day of your life."

Perhaps there is someone you know today who could be tremendously encouraged by a simple act of kindness — a telephone call, a brief note, or a short visit. Why don't you seek out that person in need today?

Do You Want to Get Even
Or Do You Want to Get Well?

I was walking down the hallway of a hospital in Birmingham when I saw an unusual sign. It read simply "Do you want to get even or do you want to get well?" As I paused to reflect upon that sign, I was reminded once again that there is a definite correlation between our emotional health and our physical health.

Ann Landers wrote, "Hate is like an acid. It does far more to the vessel in which it is stored than the object on which it is poured." Ernest Smith said, "If we live by the Old Testament law of 'an eye for an eye and a tooth for a tooth,' one day all of us will wind up one-eyed or snaggle-toothed."

We live in a world today where too many persons are paralyzed simply because they are seeking to get even. They feel as though they have been treated unjustly, and they long for the day when they can exact some sense of vengeance.

However, there comes a time in each of our lives when we must put our hurts and heartaches behind us and get on with the business of living. One of the greatest things that we can do for ourselves and our own spiritual health is to forgive and forget.

Perhaps there is something that has happened to you in the past that causes you to want to get even. It may be a trust that you made that ended in a broken relationship. It may be a business venture in which someone took advantage of you. Perhaps it is something that was said about you that was totally untrue.

If your life is paralyzed today because you want to get even, maybe you need to pause and reflect upon the same question that I saw in the corridor of the hospital in Birmingham, "Do you want to get even or do you want to get well?"

The Will of God

One of our most faithful members, Johnnie Oliver, died on December 28, 2005. She had been a member of the First United Methodist Church of Montgomery for eighty-four years, having joined Court Street Methodist in 1921. Johnnie's family members shared with me that Johnnie kept within her Bible a quotation entitled "The Will of God" that she read aloud twice each day, once in the morning and once in the afternoon. I can think of no greater spiritual discipline for each of us as we move through this fresh New Year than for each of us to read aloud this same quotation twice a day!

The will of God will never take you

      where the grace of God cannot keep you,

      where the arms of God cannot support you,

      where the riches of God cannot supply your needs,

      where the power of God cannot endow you.

The will of God will never take you

      where the Spirit of God cannot work through you,

where the wisdom of God cannot teach you,

where the army of God cannot protect you,

where the peace of God cannot calm your fears,

where the authority of God cannot overrule for you.

The will of God will never take you

where the comfort of God cannot dry your tears,

where the Word of God cannot feed you,

where the miracles of God cannot be done for you,

where the omnipresence of God cannot find you.

What I Learned from Ezell's Fish Camp

I once had the joy of speaking at the Holy Week Services at the Thomasville United Methodist Church. While I was in Thomasville, I drove over to see my mother in York. As I drove west on Highway 10, between Nanafalia and Lavaca, I turned off the highway on the west side of the Tombigbee River and drove one-half mile north to Ezell's Fish Camp. I was amazed that there was not a single sign or marker alongside the highway advertising Ezell's Fish Camp overlooking the river.

While I was enjoying my catfish I asked the waitress, "Why is it that you don't have any signs alongside the highway advertising your restaurant?"

Without cracking a smile, she said, "Everybody knows where we are located."

I was somewhat taken aback by her response, and so I asked, "What if someone like me passing through can't find your restaurant?"

Once again, with a very serious expression on her face, she said, "Well, they can always stop and ask."

When I drove away from Ezell's that day, I thought about the words that Ralph Waldo Emerson wrote long ago:

If a man can write a better book, or make a better mouse-trap than his neighbor, though he build his house in the woods, the world will make a beaten path to his door.

What is true of Ezell's Fish Camp on a Rural Route in Lavaca, Alabama, is also true of any church. Although there is a place for television, radio and newspaper advertisements, as well as directional signs to churches, there is absolutely no substitute for church members enthusiastically speaking a positive word about their church to others.

If church members say "Come and go with me to 'my' church" there are persons out there who will continue to make a beaten path to the church's door!

See Rock City!

When Clark Byers, born in Flat Rock, Alabama, was laid to rest in Trenton, Georgia, a couple of years ago, it signaled the end of one of the most amazing stories in American folk culture.

Clark Byers was working for an advertising agency in Chattanooga in 1932 when Freda Carter created Rock City atop Lookout Mountain. In an effort to attract more visitors to Rock City, Clark Byers was hired to paint promotional signs on barns alongside scenic highways from the Gulf of Mexico to the Great Lakes. He drove up and down the scenic highways, making note of the barns that he wanted to use. For renting the advertising space, the farmer got his barn painted free. Later, the farmers were paid $3.00 a year for the use of their barns.

Clark Byers painted almost 900 barns in nineteen states. He braved charging bulls, slippery roofs, and lightning bolts to paint *"See Rock City"* on top of the barns. He used a four inch brush and did all of the work freehand. His retirement closely coincided with the sounding, in the mid-1960s, of the death knell for roadway signs. This was caused by the Highway Beautification Act during the presidency of Lyndon B. Johnson.

Most of those 900 barns are now aging and crumbling, and soon the words *"See Rock City"* on old barns will be a thing of the distant past. Yet there seems to be several things about

Clark Byers and the "See Rock City" signs that we need to always remember.

1. It pays to advertise. We need to remember that as a church, the greatest and most powerful advertisement is not a painted sign on the top of an old barn, but rather a sincere spoken word shared with others. Jesus said to His disciples, "*Come . . . and you will see.*" (John 1:39)
2. There is a place for uniqueness or distinctiveness in life, whether it be an advertisement, a church, a college, a business, or even a theme park.
3. All of us need directional signs in life. Jesus said, "I am the way . . . . Follow me."

There is an old saying, "No one ever got lost on a straight road! " When we follow in the way of Jesus Christ, it is then, and only then, that we discover joy and happiness in life.

Your Luggage is in Kalamazoo, Michigan!

I was sitting in the Chicago O'Hare Airport, anxiously awaiting my flight to Memphis. I would change planes in Memphis and arrive in Montgomery at 6:30 p.m. I had spent three days in the Windy City attending a church meeting, but by Saturday afternoon, I was anxious to get home. Prior to the flight, the agent at the counter announced that the flight had been delayed for approximately two hours. When I later walked up to the counter, she also informed me that there was no way I could make my connection in Memphis and get back to Montgomery as scheduled.

Rushing down to the counter of another airline, I used a coupon for a one-way ticket home. My luggage had been checked on the previous airline, but it was evident that I would arrive in Montgomery long before my luggage did. When I got home to Montgomery, I left word at the ticket counter at Dannelly Field that I would stop by the next day to pick up my luggage. I went out to the airport early Sunday afternoon to pick up my luggage. The airline agent at the ticket counter put all of my information into the computer. He then said to me, "Your luggage is in Kalamazoo, Michigan!"

There are several responses that I wanted to make to the young man at the airline counter, simply because there were so many things in my suitcase that I desperately needed. Red Blount had invited me to give the invocation when Vice President Cheney dedicated the Blount Cultural Park on Monday, and I had in my luggage in Kalamazoo a new suit that I had planned to wear.

When I was tempted to share my anger with the young agent at the ticket counter at Dannelly Field, it suddenly dawned on me that what happened to my luggage is so typical of what happens to all of us in life. Our best-laid plans often go astray. We set out in one direction and we find ourselves going in another direction. There are all kinds of detours and interruptions in each of our lives. That is why the wise man said long ago, "Life is a diary in which we plan to write one story and are forced to write another."

In light of this, it seems that the people who handle life the best are those who remember that detours and interruptions are an inevitable part of life. Yet, even in the midst of all of our detours and interruptions, God can work out His redeeming purposes.

Incidentally, does anyone know where Kalamazoo, Michigan, is located? Even better, does anyone have a relative or friend in Kalamazoo who could help me retrieve my luggage?

A Religion for the Birds

The migration of birds has always had a strange fascination for me. We are told that many birds fly thousands of miles across the oceans each year only to return to the very same birdhouses from which they departed. I find it thrilling to pause and consider that God in His infinite wisdom would create these feathered creatures with such a marvelous sense of direction. Surely a God who cares for such, the lowliest of creatures, does not forget us when we seek His direction in life.

Jesus reminded His hearers that a sparrow could not fall in flight without His knowledge. The knowledge of such a caring and loving God who watches over us day and night is a constant source of inspiration to me.

Bishop Quayle told the story of a night that he was unable to sleep. As he was tossing and turning in bed, he decided to get up and read his Bible. As he opened his Bible, he read these words of Psalm 121, "*He that keepeth Israel shall neither slumber nor sleep.*" (Psalm 121:4 KJV)

In that moment, he heard the voice of God saying, "Quayle, there is no need for both of us to stay up all night long. I am going to be up anyway. Why don't you go back to bed and get some sleep?" Bishop Quayle said that he went back to bed and fell sound asleep.

John Greenleaf Whittier in *The Eternal Goodness* expressed it best:

> I know not what the future hath
> of marvel or surprise;
> Assured alone that life and death,
> His mercy underlies.
>
> I know not where His islands lift
> their fronded palms in air;
> I only know I cannot drift
> beyond His love and care.

Living in Hurtsboro

There is an interesting little town in southeast Russell County called Hurtsboro. Some of the nicest people I have ever met live in that small town, but the town has always had a strange fascination for me, simply because of its name.

All of us at some point in our lives live in Hurtsboro. I have discovered in my own Christian pilgrimage that "Everybody hurts somewhere." All of us have our hidden scars that have come as a result of the hurts and heartaches of life.

Leo Buscaglia told the story of the man who sent to twenty-five of his slight acquaintances, whose names he picked at random, a note with the very same message, "I just wanted you to know that I am thinking of you today in your difficult situation."

Would you believe that the man received twenty-five prompt replies thanking him for his thoughtfulness!

Ian MacClaren once said "Let us be kind to one another, for most of us are fighting a hard battle."

Most people with whom we come into contact day by day are fighting difficult battles. We as Christians need to be kind to one another, tenderhearted, forgiving one another, even as God in Jesus Christ has forgiven us.

Perhaps there is someone near you today who needs to hear a word of encouragement, a sincere expression of thanksgiving, or maybe that person needs to see a deed of kindness. As a church we need to reach out to those who hurt and say genuinely, "What happens to you makes a difference to me."

The Art of Appreciation

James Michener, the famous novelist, was named the "Philanthropist of the Year" not long ago by the National Society of Fund Raising Executives. My daughter Carmen and I attended the banquet in Los Angeles where the announcement was made.

The person making the presentation revealed that James Michener had given his alma mater two million dollars. In so doing, Michener said that he was repaying a $2,000 scholarship which he had received as a student, with one million, nine hundred and ninety-eight thousand dollars interest!

I am sure there were many cynics who said "Well, he could afford it!" However, I continue to be impressed with people who choose to do what they can afford to do. I think it is a beautiful thing for someone to look at a small thing which was done for him or her somewhere along the way and feel such appreciation that his or her response is out of proportion to what was received.

When the Major League Baseball Hall of Fame held its induction ceremony not long ago in Cooperstown, New York, a longtime sportscaster asked Rod Carew, one of the inductees, to describe the difference between the "old-timers" and the players of today.

I was very much intrigued with his response. He did not say anything about physical differences or athletic skills. He simply said, "The 'old-timers' were much more appreciative!"

When our society has "*progressed*" or "*regressed*" to the point where former major league players can demand large sums of money from children for simply autographing baseball cards, it calls into serious question where we are headed as a nation. "Autograph parties" where athletes demand fees from the very individuals who are personally responsible for lifting them up to their lofty status in life raise all kinds of questions.

Perhaps Elizabeth Bibesco was right on target: "Blessed are those who can receive without forgetting, and can give without remembering!"

The Sand in Our Shoes

Several years ago, a young man by the name of Peter Jenkins came through Montgomery on his *"walk across America."* He stayed in the home of two of our wonderful church members, Gloria and Jordan Walker. When Peter came with them to church he told me that he was working with *National Geographic*, had left his home in New York, and was spending several weeks in Montgomery before moving on to Mobile and then westward to California. Little did I realize during the times that he worshiped with us and we talked together that his book *Walk Across America* would become the number one best-seller on the *New York Times* best-seller list!

Whenever I think about Peter Jenkins' "walk across America" I always think of the man who made a similar trek several years ago. When he finally reached the coast of California and placed his tired feet in the Pacific Ocean members of the news media were present to ask him a number of questions. As you would anticipate they asked him, "What was the most difficult part of your trip? What was the biggest obstacle that you faced along the way? Was it the hot, sandy deserts? Was it the difficult terrain of the mountains? Was it the rivers you had to cross?"

Much to the surprise of his hearers the man said, "No, it was none of these things. The most difficult part was the sand in my shoes!"

Most of us are able to cope with the "big" things of life — hardship, tragedy, and sorrow. Most of the time we can handle major traumas with dignity and strength. However, too many lives are torn apart by the little, irritating things in life like "the sand in our shoes."

Let us not overlook the little irritating things of life that have a way of doing great damage.

Love, Medicine, and Miracles

I love the story of the man who was filling out an application form for a job. When he came to the question "Who to call in case of an accident? "the applicant filled in the blank, "Anyone in sight!"

When we are hurting, all of us desperately long for someone within sight or sound of our voice to pause long enough to care.

One of the most popular books in America several years ago was a book entitled *Love, Medicine, and Miracles.* Author Dr. Bernie Siegel practices surgery in New Haven, Connecticut, but he also teaches at Yale University. Dr. Siegel contends that miracles are happening every day to patients who have the courage to work with their doctors to participate in and influence their own recovery. He reminds us that there is far more to medicine than pills and incisions. He claims that there is a definite relationship between attitude and disease, that our state of mind has an immediate and direct effect upon our state of body.

Dr. Siegel strongly emphasizes that a loving, caring, compassionate attitude towards another person can drastically improve that person's chances for healing and wholeness in life.

247

Dr. Siegel shares the story of the research done by Dr. Lawrence Egbert at Harvard University. In his research, Dr. Egbert discovered that patients who received a visit from the anesthesiologist the night before surgery, as well as other explanations and reassurances, needed *only half* as much pain medication and left the hospital two-and-a-half days sooner than those who did not receive any explanations or reassurances.

Sir William Osler, the famous Canadian physician, once said "The outcome of tuberculosis had more to do with what went on in the patient's mind than what went on in his lungs."

Perhaps there is someone you know today that could experience healing and wholeness in his life if you showed that person you really cared. How true is it that "people do not care how much we know until they know how much we care!"

A Lesson from the Bumblebee

In the briefing rooms of American air bases during World War II there were posters that contained the following inscription:

By all the known laws of which can be proved on paper or in the wind tunnel, the bumblebee cannot fly.

The size of his wings in relation to his body, according to aeronautical and mathematical science, simply means that he cannot fly. It is an impossibility.

But of course the bumblebee does not know about these rules, and so he goes ahead and flies anyway.

Perhaps there is a lesson that all of us can learn from the bumblebee. I wonder what would happen if we focused each day on our "possibilities" rather than our "impossibilities." I dare say that we would most likely achieve our goals. The late Dr. Karl Menninger of the Menninger Institute in Topeka, Kansas, reminded us that "attitudes are far more important than ancestors."

The Apostle Paul, writing to the Philippians (4:13) said, *"I can do everything through Him who gives me strength."*

Dr. Norman Vincent Peale, author of *The Power of Positive Thinking*, reminded us that if we would repeat that one verse aloud ten times each day, it would change our lives.

Are you focusing on your "possibilities" or "impossibilities?" Let us approach each day with the confidence that we can overcome all obstacles with the strength that Christ will give.

Disturb Us, Lord!

Charles and Elaine McDonald, two of our most faithful members, attended the confirmation service for their granddaughter, Leslie Warren, that was held several months ago in Savannah, Georgia. While worshiping at St. Peter's Episcopal Church that day, they discovered the following poem in a brochure that welcomed them to the church.

Disturb us, Lord, when we are too well pleased with ourselves,
When our dreams have come true because we dreamed too little,
When we arrive safely because we sailed too close to the shore.

Disturb us, Lord, when, with the abundance of things we possess,
We have lost our thirst for the waters of life;
Having fallen in love with life, we have ceased to dream of eternity.
And in our efforts to build a new earth,
We have allowed our vision of the new Heaven to dim.

Disturb us, Lord, to dare more boldly,

251

To venture on wider seas, where storms will show
your mastery;
Where losing sight of land, we shall find stars.
We ask you to push back the horizons of our hopes,
And to push us in the future in strength, courage,
hope, and love.

This we ask in the name of our Captain, who is Jesus
Christ. Amen.

May our prayer this week be, "Disturb us, Lord, when
we become too complacent and comfortable!"

Are You Looking for Change in Others?

Dr. Cecil Osborne of Yokefellows spoke at our Blue Lake Assembly Ground several years ago. As the author of a book entitled *Understanding Your Mate*, Dr. Osborne said that all couples getting married need to memorize one universal law that has three parts:

1. I can never change another person by direct action.
2. I can only change myself.
3. When I change the way I think and feel and act, others tend to change in relationship with me.

Perhaps that universal law could apply to every aspect of our lives. While we cannot change other persons by direct action, we can do something even more effective and that is, we can change ourselves. If we change ourselves, we will discover that others will change in relationship to us.

One of the great prayers of the Bible is found within the 139th Psalm, *"Search me, O God, and know my heart; test me and know my anxious thoughts. See if there is any offensive way in me, and lead me in the way everlasting."* (Psalm 139:23-24)

What changes do you want to make within your own life? There is no better time to make these changes than today!

Today

One of our most faithful members, Edna Earle Eich, died on March 21, 2004. Family members shared with me that Edna Earle always displayed in a very conspicuous place within her home the words of Alfred A. Montapert.

She read these words every single day! Perhaps all of us would live fuller lives if we did the same!

This is the beginning of a fresh new day.
I greet it with hope.
Today comes only once, and never again returns.
I must show my love and be kind.
God has given me this twenty-four hours
to use as I will.
I shall have a cheerful attitude.

I must do something good with this day
and not waste it.
This is my day of opportunity and duty,
I expect something good
because I am going to make it happen.

Today is a new day in my life,
a new piece of road to be traveled,
I must ask God for directions.

Today I will be filled with courage and confidence,
I must show my faith in God.

254

What I do today is very important
because I am exchanging a day of my life for it.
The cost of a thing is the amount of my life
I spend obtaining it.

When tomorrow comes,
leaving in its place something I have traded for it.

In order not to forget the price I paid for it,
I shall do my best to make it
useful, profitable, joyful.

The seeds I plant today
determine my harvest in the future.
My life will be richer or poorer
by the way I use today.

Thank you, God, for today.
I shall not pass this way again —

What I must do — I'll do today!